BY THE SAME AUTHOR:

ARRABAL

PLAYS VOLUME 1

ORISON
THE TWO EXECUTIONERS
FANDO AND LIS
THE CAR CEMETERY

TRANSLATED BY BARBARA WRIGHT

JOHN CALDER
LONDON

First published in Great Britain 1962 by John Calder (Publishers) Ltd
18 Brewer Street, London W1R 4AS.

Reprinted March 1976

© copyright English Translation, John Calder (Publishers), 1962
© copyright French text, Rene Julliard, 1958

ISBN 07145 0449 1 cased
ISBN 07145 0450 5 paper

Printed by Unwin Brothers Limited, Gresham Press,
Old Woking, Surrey.

CONTENTS

ORISON

A Mystical Play

ON THE STAGE

The two Characters: FIDIO and LILBÉ *(Man and Woman)*
A child's coffin (black)
Four candles
An iron Crucifix
At the back of the stage, a black curtain.

The play has only one scene.

Music in the distance: Louis Armstrong's "Black and Blue."
Silence.

FIDIO. From today on we're going to be good and pure.

LILBÉ. What's come over you?

FIDIO. I say that from today on we're going to be good and pure, like the angels.

LILBÉ. Us?

FIDIO. Yes.

LILBÉ. We couldn't be.

FIDIO. You're right. *(Pause.)* It'll be very difficult. *(Pause.)* We'll try.

LILBÉ. How?

FIDIO. By keeping God's laws.

LILBÉ. I've forgotten them.

FIDIO. So have I.

LILBÉ. How'll we manage, then?

FIDIO. To know what's good or bad?

LILBÉ. Yes.

FIDIO. I've bought a Bible.

LILBÉ. Is that all we need?

FIDIO. Yes, that'll be all we'll need.

LILBÉ. We'll be saints.

FIDIO. That would be too much to ask. *(Pause.)* But we can try.

LILBÉ. Everything will be completely different.

FIDIO. Yes, very.

LILBÉ. But then we won't be bored, like we are now.

FIDIO. And it'll be very nice, too.

LILBÉ. Are you sure?

FIDIO. Yes, of course.

LILBÉ. Read me a bit of the book.

FIDIO. The Bible?

LILBÉ. Yes.

FIDIO *(reading)*. "In the beginning God created the heaven and the earth." *(Enthusiastically.)* Isn't that nice?

LILBÉ. Yes, it's very nice.

FIDIO *(reading)*. "And God said, Let there be light: and there was light. And God saw the light, that it was good: and God divided the light from the darkness. And God called the light Day, and the darkness he called Night. And the evening and the morning were the first day."

LILBÉ. Is that how everything started?

FIDIO. Yes. You see how simple it is, and how beautiful.

LILBÉ. Yes, it sounded much more complicated when I heard about it before.

FIDIO. The story of the cosmos?

LILBÉ *(smiling)*. Yes.

FIDIO *(smiling)*. It did to me, too.

LILBÉ *(smiling)*. And evolution, too.

FIDIO. What a business!

LILBÉ. Read me a bit more.

FIDIO *(reading)*. "And the Lord God formed man of the dust of the ground, and breathed into his nostrils the breath of life; and man became a living soul." *(Pause.)* "And the Lord God caused a deep sleep to fall upon Adam, and he slept; and he took one of his ribs, and closed up the flesh instead thereof; and the rib, which the Lord God had taken from man, made he a woman."

Fidio and Lilbé kiss.

LILBÉ *(anxiously)*. And shall we be able to sleep together like we used to?

FIDIO. No.

LILBÉ. Shall I have to sleep all by myself, then?

FIDIO. Yes.

LILBÉ. But I'll be awfully cold.

FIDIO. You'll get used to it.

LILBÉ. What about you? Won't you be cold?

FIDIO. Yes, I will too.

LILBÉ. Then we shan't argue, like when you take all the blankets?

FIDIO. 'Course not.

LILBÉ. It's a bit tricky being good.

FIDIO. Yes, very.

LILBÉ. Shall I be allowed to tell lies?

FIDIO. No.

LILBÉ. Not even very little ones?

FIDIO. Not even those.

LILBÉ. Nor steal oranges from the grocer?

FIDIO. Not any more.

LILBÉ. Shan't we be able to enjoy ourselves, like we used to, in the cemetery?

FIDIO. Yes, why shouldn't we?

LILBÉ. And how about poking out dead people's eyes, like we used to?

FIDIO. No, not that.

LILBÉ. And what about killing people?

FIDIO. No.

LILBÉ. Well then, are we going to let people go on living?

FIDIO. Obviously.

LILBÉ. Ah well, they'll have to put up with it.

FIDIO. Don't you realise what you have to do to be good?

LILBÉ. No. *(Pause.)* Do you?

FIDIO. Not very clearly. *(Pause.)* But I've got the book, so I'll be able to find out.

LILBÉ. Still the book.

FIDIO. Still the book.

LILBÉ. And then what'll happen?

FIDIO. We'll go to heaven.

LILBÉ. Both of us?

FIDIO. If we both behave ourselves, yes.

LILBÉ. And what'll we do in heaven?

FIDIO. We'll enjoy ourselves.

LILBÉ. All the time?

FIDIO. Yes, all the time.

LILBÉ *(incredulous)*. It's not possible.

FIDIO. Yes it is; it *is* possible.

LILBÉ. Why?

FIDIO. Because God is all-powerful. God does impossible things. Miracles.

LILBÉ. Well I never!

FIDIO. And in the simplest possible way.

LILBÉ. If I were he I'd do the same.

FIDIO. Listen to what the Bible says: "And they bring a blind man unto Him, and besought Him to touch him. And He took the blind man by the hand, and led him out of the town; and when He had spit on his eyes, and put His hands upon him, He asked him if he saw ought. And he looked up and said, I see men as trees, walking. After that He put His hands again upon his eyes and made him look up, and he was restored, and saw every man clearly."

LILBÉ. Isn't that nice.

FIDIO. He said that we must be good.

LILBÉ. Then we'll be good.

FIDIO. And that we must become as little children.

LILBÉ. Be like children?

FIDIO. Yes, as pure as children.

LILBÉ. That's difficult.

FIDIO. We'll try.

LILBÉ. Why have you suddenly taken up this craze?

FIDIO. I've had enough.

LILBÉ. Is that the only reason?

FIDIO. And anyway, what we'd been doing up to now was horrible. This is much nicer.

LILBÉ. And what's all that stuff about heaven?

FIDIO. That's where we'll go when we're dead.

LILBÉ. Not till then?

FIDIO. No.

LILBÉ. Can't we go there before?

FIDIO. No.

LILBÉ. That's not much fun.

FIDIO. Yes, that's the worst of it.

LILBÉ. And what'll we do in heaven?

FIDIO. I've already told you : we shall enjoy ourselves.

LILBÉ. I'd like to hear you say that again. *(Pause.)* It doesn't seem possible.

FIDIO. We shall be like the angels.

LILBÉ. Like the good ones or like the other ones?

FIDIO. The other ones don't go to heaven; the other ones are devils and they go to hell.

LILBÉ. And what do they do there?

FIDIO. They suffer a lot : they get burnt.

LILBÉ. That makes a change!

FIDIO. Those angels are very wicked and they've rebelled against God.

LILBÉ. Why?

FIDIO. Pride. They wanted to be exalted above God.

LILBÉ. That was going a bit far.

FIDIO. Yes, a lot too far.

LILBÉ. But *we*'ll be satisfied with a lot less than that.

FIDIO. Yes, a lot less.

LILBÉ. You know, I feel like starting to be good straight-away.

FIDIO. We'll start this very minute.

LILBÉ. Just like that, without any fuss?

FIDIO. Yes.

LILBÉ. Nobody'll notice.

FIDIO. Yes they will, God will notice.

LILBÉ. Are you sure?

FIDIO. Yes, God sees everything.

LILBÉ. Does he even see when I have a pee?

FIDIO. Yes, even that.

LILBÉ. I'll be ashamed, now.

FIDIO. God writes down everything good that you do in gold letters in a very beautiful book and all your sins in a very ugly book in very ugly writing.

LILBÉ. I'll be good. I want Him always to write in gold letters.

FIDIO. That oughtn't to be the only reason for you to be good.

LILBÉ. Why else should I be?

FIDIO. To behold felicity.

LILBÉ. What on earth do you mean? To behold felicity?

FIDIO. To be happy.

LILBÉ. Will I be able to be happy too, when I'm good?

FIDIO. Yes, that too.

LILBÉ. Does felicity exist?

FIDIO. Yes. *(Pause.)* So they say.

LILBÉ *(sadly)*. And what about the things we used to do?

FIDIO. The bad things we used to do?

LILBÉ. Yes.

FIDIO. We'll have to confess them.

LILBÉ. All of them?

FIDIO. Yes, all of them.

LILBÉ. And about how you undress me so's your friends can sleep with me?

FIDIO. Yes, that too.

LILBÉ. And . . . that we're murderers? *(She points to the coffin.)*

FIDIO. Yes, that too. *(Pause. Sadly.)* We oughtn't to have killed it. *(Pause.)* We're wicked. We must be good.

LILBÉ *(Sadly)*. We killed it for the same reason.

FIDIO. The same reason?

LILBÉ. Yes, we killed it because we wanted to enjoy ourselves.

FIDIO. Yes.

LILBÉ. And we only enjoyed ourselves for a moment.

Fidio. Yes.

Lilbé. If we try to be good, it won't be like it was before, will it?

Fidio. No, it'll be more complete.

Lilbé. More complete?

Fidio. And nicer.

Lilbé. And nicer?

Fidio. Yes, you know how the Son of God was born? *(Pause.)* It happened a long time ago. He was born in a very poor manger in Bethlehem and as He didn't have any money to keep Himself warm, an ox and an ass warmed Him up with their breath. And as the ox was terribly pleased to be serving God it went moo moo. And the ass brayed. And the baby's mother, who was the mother of God, cried, and her husband cheered her up.

Lilbé. I like that very much.

Fidio. So do I.

Lilbé. And what happened to the baby?

Fidio. He didn't say a word, even though He was God. And as the people were unkind they hardly gave Him anything to eat.

Lilbé. What awful people.

Fidio. But one day in a kingdom a long way off, some Kings, who were very good men, saw a moving star stuck up in the sky. They followed it.

Lilbé. Who were they, those Kings?

Fidio. They were Melchior, Gaspar and Balthazar.

Lilbé. The ones who put toys in your stocking at Christmas?

B

FIDIO. Yes. *(Pause.)* And they were following and following the star, and finally one day they arrived at the manger in Bethlehem. So they gave the child everything they had brought on their camels : a lot of toys, and sweets, and some chocolate too. *(Pause. They smile enthusiastically.)* Oh, yes, I was forgetting, they gave Him some gold and myrrh and frankincense, too.

LILBÉ. What a lot of things !

FIDIO. And so the child was very pleased, and so were His parents, and the ox and the ass too.

LILBÉ. And then what happened?

FIDIO. Then the child helped His father, who was a carpenter, to make tables and chairs. As He was a very good boy his mother often used to kiss Him.

LILBÉ. He was different from most children.

FIDIO. He was God.

LILBÉ. Oh, yes, so He was. . . .

FIDIO. The good thing about Him, though, was that He didn't do any miracles just so as to have nice things to eat, or to buy expensive clothes.

LILBÉ. And what happened?

FIDIO. Afterwards He became a man, but the Jews were horrid and killed Him; they crucified Him, with nails in His hands and feet. Can you imagine it?

LILBÉ *(pleased)*. That must have hurt a lot.

FIDIO. Yes, a lot.

LILBÉ. He must have cried a lot.

FIDIO. No, not at all. He didn't let himself. And another thing, to make Him look more ridiculous they put Him between two thieves.

LILBÉ. Nasty thieves or nice ones?

FIDIO. Nasty ones, the worst ones, the two nastiest ones they could find.

LILBÉ. Oh, that's bad!

FIDIO. Mm! And then what's more it turned out that one of the two thieves was a kind of impostor! A chap who deceived his own people.

LILBÉ. Who deceived his own people?

FIDIO. Yes, he'd made out that he was bad and then all of a sudden they discovered that he was good.

LILBÉ. And what happened?

FIDIO. Well, God died on the cross.

LILBÉ. Did He?

FIDIO. Yes. But He rose again on the third day.

LILBÉ *(pleased)*. Goodness!

FIDIO. And then everybody realised that He'd been telling the truth.

LILBÉ *(enthusiastically)*. I want to be good.

FIDIO. So do I.

LILBÉ. Straightaway.

FIDIO. Yes, straightaway.

LILBÉ. I want to be like the child who was born in the manger.

FIDIO. So do I.

Fidio takes Lilbés hands in his own.

LILBÉ *(worried)*. And what shall we do all day long?

Fidio. Good deeds.

Lilbé. All the time?

Fidio. Well, nearly all the time.

Lilbé. And the rest of the time?

Fidio. We could go to the zoo.

Lilbé. To watch the monkeys doing you know what?

Fidio. No. *(Pause.)* To see the hens and the pigeons.

Lilbé. And what else can we do?

Fidio. We can play the ocarina?

Lilbé. The ocarina?

Fidio. Yes.

Lilbé. All right. *(Pause.)* Isn't that wicked?

Fidio *(thinking)*. No, I don't think so.

Lilbé. And what'll we have to do to be really good?

Fidio. I'll tell you. If we see that something annoys someone, we won't do it. If we see that something would
please someone we'll do it. If we see that someone is poor and
old and paralysed and he hasn't any friends, well, we'll go
and visit him.

Lilbé. We won't kill him?

Fidio. No!

Lilbé. Poor old man!

Fidio. But you don't seem to understand that we can't kill
people any more.

Lilbé. Oh! Go on.

FIDIO. If we see a woman carrying something heavy, we'll help her. *(A judge's voice.)* If we see someone committing an injustice, we'll put it right.

LILBÉ. Injustices as well?

FIDIO. Yes, those as well.

LILBÉ *(satisfied)*. We're going to be very important people.

FIDIO. Yes, very.

LILBÉ *(worried)*. And how shall we know whether it *is* an injustice?

FIDIO. We'll just guess.

Silence.

LILBÉ. That'll be a bore.

Silence. Fidio is discouraged.

It's going to be just like everything else.

Silence.

We'll get tired of being good, too.

Silence.

FIDIO. But we'll try.

In the distance, Louis Armstrong's "Black and Blue" is heard.

Curtain

THE TWO EXECUTIONERS

Melodrama in One Act

CHARACTERS

The Two Executioners, I don't know their names
The Mother, FRANÇOISE
The Two Sons, BENOÎT and MAURICE
The Husband, JEAN

The action takes place in a very dark room. Left, a door open-ing on to the road. At the back, the door which gives on to the torture chamber. Bare walls. In the middle of the room, a table and three chairs.

It is dark. The two executioners are alone, sitting on the chairs. There is an insistent knock at the street door. It really looks as if the executioners can't hear anything. The door opens slowly, not without creaking. A woman's head appears. The woman inspects the room. She decides to come in and goes up to the executioners.

FRANÇOISE. Good morning gentlemen. . . . Excuse me. . . . Am I disturbing you?

The executioners remain motionless, as if it was nothing to do with them.

If I'm disturbing you I'll go away. . . .

Silence. It looks as if the woman is trying to pluck up courage. Finally she brings herself to speak and the words come tumbling out.

I came to see you because I can't stand it any longer. It's about my husband. *(Pathetically.)* The being in whom I placed all my hopes, the man to whom I gave the best years of my life and whom I loved as I would never have thought I could love. *(Speaking more softly, calmer.)* Yes, yes, yes, he is guilty.

Suddenly the executioners take an interest in what the woman is saying. One of them takes out a pencil and notebook.

Yes, he's guilty. He lives at No. 8 rue du Travail, and his name is Jean Lagune.

The executioner makes a note of it. As soon as he has done so the executioners go out by the street door. A car is heard driving off. Françoise also goes out by the street door.

VOICE OF FRANÇOISE. Come in, children, come in.

VOICE OF BENOÎT. There's not much light here.

VOICE OF FRANÇOISE. Yes, the room is very dark. It frightens me, but we must go in. We've got to wait for Daddy.

Enter Françoise and her two sons, Benoît and Maurice.

FRANÇOISE. Sit down, children. Don't be afraid.

All three sit down round the table.

FRANÇOISE *(she always speaks in a whining voice)*. What sad and dramatic moments we are living through! What sins are we guilty of, that life should punish us so cruelly?

BENOÎT. Don't worry, Mother. Don't cry.

FRANÇOISE. No, my son, I'm not crying, I shan't cry, I shall stand up to all the dangers that beset us. How I love to see you always so solicitous about everything that concerns me! But just look at your brother Maurice—as unnatural as ever.

Maurice, with a melancholy air, looks apparently deliberately in the opposite direction from his mother.

Look at him; today, when more than ever I need your support, he turns against me and overwhelms me with scorn. What harm have I ever done you, unworthy son? Speak to me, say something.

BENOÎT. Don't take any notice of him, Mother, he doesn't know anything about the gratitude one owes to a mother.

FRANÇOISE *(to Maurice)*. Can't you hear your brother? Listen to him. If anyone said such a thing to me I'd die of shame. But *you* aren't ashamed. Good God! What a cross!

BENOÎT. Gently, Mother, don't let him upset you. He'll never agree with you.

FRANÇOISE. Yes, my son, you don't realise. When it isn't your father, it's Maurice: nothing but suffering. And when I've always been their slave. Just look what a gay life so many women of my age lead, enjoying themselves night and day going to dances, cafés, cinemas! So many women! You can't realise it properly, you're still too young. I could have done the same, but I preferred to sacrifice myself for my husband and for you, silently, humbly, without expecting anything from my sacrifices, and even knowing that one day the beings who have been the dearest to me would say what your brother says today—that I haven't done enough. Can you see, my son, how they reward my sacrifices? You can see—by always returning evil for good, always.

BENOÎT. How good you are! How good you are!

FRANÇOISE. But what good does it do me to know that? It comes to the same thing. Everything comes to the same thing. I don't feel like doing anything any more, I don't care about anything, nothing is important to me any more. I just want to be good and always sacrifice myself for you, without expecting anything for my sacrifices, and even knowing that one day the beings who have been the dearest to me, those who ought to be grateful for all my concern for them, deliberately ignore my sacrifices. All my life I've been a martyr to you, and I shall continue to be a martyr until God chooses to recall me to Him.

BENOÎT. Dearest Mother!

FRANÇOISE. Yes, my son, I live only for you. How can I have any other interests? Luxury, dresses, parties, the theatre —none of these count for me, I have but one care : you. What does the rest matter?

BENOÎT (to Maurice). Maurice, do you hear what Mother says?

FRANÇOISE. Let him be, my child. Do you think I can hope that he will be able to recognise my sacrifices? No. I expect nothing from him. I even know that he probably thinks that I haven't done enough.

BENOÎT (to Maurice). You're a good-for-nothing.

FRANÇOISE *(excited)*. Don't make things worse for me, Benoît, don't pick a quarrel with him. I want us to live in peace, in harmony. Whatever happens I don't want you brothers to quarrel.

BENOÎT. How good you are, Mother! . . and good to him when he's so worthless. If it weren't for the fact that you ask me to spare him, I don't know what I'd do to him. *(To Maurice, aggressively)*. You can say thank you to Mother, Maurice, because you deserve a good thrashing.

FRANÇOISE. No, my child, no, don't hit him. I don't want you to hit him even if he does thoroughly deserve it. I want peace and love to reign in our midst. That's the only thing I ask of you, Benoît.

BENOÎT. Don't worry, I'll do what you ask.

FRANÇOISE. Thank you, my son. You are like balm for the injuries that life has inflicted upon me. You see, God in his infinite goodness has finally granted me a son like you to bind up the wounds my poor heart suffers, the grief caused me, to my great distress, by the beings I have struggled for the most : my husband and Maurice.

BENOÎT *(angrily)*. From now on, no one shall make you suffer any more.

FRANÇOISE. Don't be angry, my son, don't be upset. They've behaved badly, and they know it. What we must do is forgive them, and bear them no malice. And anyway, even though your father has sinned, sinned greatly even, you must nonetheless respect him.

BENOÎT. Respect him : *him*?

FRANÇOISE. Yes, my son. You must disregard all the sufferings he has caused. It is I who should refuse him my forgiveness, and you see, my son, I forgive him, although he has made me suffer more than I have suffered before, if that is possible,

I shall continue to wait for him with open arms and I shall be able to forgive him his innumerable faults. Ever since the day I was born, life has taught me how to suffer. But I carry this cross with dignity, out of love for you.

BENOÎT. Mother, you're so good!

FRANÇOISE *(in an even more humble tone)*. I try, Benoît, to be good.

BENOÎT *(interrupting his mother with a gesture of spontanious affection)*. Mother, you are the best woman in the world.

FRANÇOISE *(humble and ashamed)*. No, my son, I am not the best woman in the world, I cannot aspire to such a claim, I am too unworthy. And then, I have probably committed some sins. In spite of a great deal of good will; but even so, what counts is that I have committed some sins.

BENOÎT *(with conviction)*. No, Mother; never.

FRANÇOISE. Yes, my child, sometimes. But I can say with joy that I have always repented of them—always.

BENOÎT. You are a saint.

FRANÇOISE. Hush! What more beautiful dream could I have than saintliness! I can't be a saint. To be a saint one must be a very great person, but I am worth nothing. I simply try to be good—that is the limit of my pretensions.

The street door opens. Enter the two executioners, carrying Jean, Françoise's husband, who has his feet and wrists tied together and is hanging from a big stick, rather after the fashion in which captured lions or tigers are carried in Africa. Jean is gagged; as he is brought into the room he raises his head and looks at his wife, Françoise, opening his eyes very widely and perhaps with some anger. Françoise looks at her husband attentively, avidly even. Maurice watches the procession go by with violent indignation. The two executioners, without stopping, cross the room and carry Jean from the street door into the torture chamber. All three disappear.

MAURICE *(to his mother, very indignantly)*. What's going on? What's the latest dirty trick?

BENOÎT *(to Maurice)*. Don't talk to Mother like that.

FRANÇOISE. Let him be, my child, let him insult me. Let him reproach me. Let him treat his mother like an enemy. Let him be, my child, let him be, God will punish this wicked action.

MAURICE. Oh, that's *too* much. *(Angrily, to his mother.)* It was you who denounced him.

BENOÎT *(ready to throw himself on his brother)*. I've already told you to speak civilly to Mother. D'you understand? Civilly! D'you hear me?

FRANÇOISE. Gently, my son, gently, let him be rude to me. You know very well that he's only happy when he's making me suffer; give him that satisfaction. That's my job—to sacrifice myself for him and for you; to give you everything you want.

BENOÎT. I won't let him shout at you.

FRANÇOISE. Obey me, my son, obey me.

BENOÎT. I won't obey you. You're too good and he takes advantage of it.

Maurice looks dejected.

FRANÇOISE. My child, do you too want to make me suffer? If he is unpleasant to me, let him be unpleasant, it was only to be expected, but you, my son, you are different—at least that's what I've always thought. Let him torture me if it does his evil heart any good.

BENOÎT. No, never; not when I'm there, at any rate.

The sounds of a whip can be heard, followed by cries muffled by the gag. It is Jean. The executioners are, no doubt, flogging him in the torture chamber. Françoise and Maurice get up and go over to the torture chamber door. The mother listens avidly, her eyes wide open, a grimace on her face (almost a smile?), hysterical. The sounds of the whip become louder for a long moment. Jean groans loudly. At last the sounds of the whip and the cries cease.

MAURICE *(furiously, and on the verge of tears, to his mother)*. It's your fault that they're whipping Daddy. It was you who denounced him.

BENOÎT. Shut up! *(violently.)* Don't take any notice, Mother.

FRANÇOISE. Let him be, let him be, Benoît. Let him insult me. I know very well that if you weren't there he would hit me. But he's a coward and he's afraid of you, that's the only thing that stops him, because he is quite capable of lifting his hand against his mother, I can read it in his eyes. He's always been trying to.

A piercing moan from Jean. Silence. Françoise makes a grimace which is almost a smile. Silence.

Let's go and see poor little Daddy. Let's go and see him suffering, the poor man. Because there's no doubt about it, they must have hurt him a lot.

Grimaces from Françoise. Silence. Françoise approaches the torture chamber, half-opens the door and, standing by the door, looks into the room.

(talking to her husband, who is in the room and so can't see her). They must have hurt you a lot, Jean. Poor Jean! You must have suffered so much, and they're going to make you suffer even more. My poor Jean!

Jean, though impeded by the gag, cries out in anger.

Don't get into a state. It'd be better to try to be patient. You must realise that you're only at the beginning of your sufferings. You can't do anything at the moment, you're tied up, and your back's covered with blood. You can't do anything. Just calm down! And anyway, all this is going to do you a lot of good, it'll teach you to have some will power—you never did have any.

Françoise decides to go into the room; she does so, i.e. she goes off-stage.

VOICE OF FRANÇOISE *(speaking as if she were at church, but out loud).* It was I who denounced you, Jean. It was I who said you were guilty.

Jean tries to speak, but as he is hindered by his gag he can only manage to make noises. Françoise's abnormal laugh can be heard. Maurice is very worked up. Françoise reappears.

FRANÇOISE *(to her sons).* The poor man is suffering a lot, he hasn't any patience, he never did have any.

Cry from Jean.

MAURICE. Leave Daddy alone. Don't go on. Can't you see you're tormenting him?

FRANÇOISE. It's he who's tormenting himself; only he, and for no reason. *(She again addresses her husband through the door.)* I can see very well that it's you who are tormenting yourself. I can see very well that what I say irritates you. *(Pause—smile.)* Who could pay more attention to your sufferings than I do? I shall be at your side every time you suffer. You're guilty, and it's your duty to accept your punishment with patience. You even ought to thank the executioners for taking so much trouble with you. If you were a normal, humble, just man, you'd thank the executioners, but you've always been a rebel. You needn't think you're at home now, at home where you did everything you wanted to; at the moment you're in the executioners' power. Accept your punishment without rebelling. It's your purification. Repent your sins, and promise that you won't fall back into error. And don't torment yourself with the thought that I am rejoicing to see you punished.

Loud groan from Jean.

MAURICE. Can't you hear him groaning? Can't you see you're making him suffer? Leave him in peace!

BENOÎT. I've already told you not to talk to Mother like that.

FRANÇOISE. Let him talk to me as he wishes, my son. I'm used to it. It's my lot: to worry about them, about him and about Daddy, though they don't deserve it, and though no one thanks me for it.

Groans from Jean.

MAURICE. Daddy! Daddy! *(On the verge of tears.)* Daddy!

FRANÇOISE. He's still groaning. That's a sign that he's suffering from the wounds caused by the whip and the ropes fastening his hands and feet. *(She opens the drawer in the table and searches about inside it. Then she puts on the table a bottle of vinegar and a salt cellar which she has found in it.)* These are just what I need. I'll put vinegar and salt on his wounds to disinfect them. A bit of vinegar and salt on his wounds will do wonders! *(With hysterical enthusiasm.)* A bit of salt and vinegar. Only just a tiny bit on each wound, that's all he needs.

MAURICE *(angrily)*. Don't do that.

FRANÇOISE. Is that the way you love your father? You, his favourite son, is that how you treat him? You, you of all people, wicked son! You who know very well that the executioners will flog him until death results, are you going to abandon him now and not even let me bandage his wounds?

Françoise goes towards the torture chamber with the vinegar and salt in her hand.

MAURICE. Don't put salt on him! If they're going to kill him anyway, at least leave him in peace, don't make the agony worse.

FRANÇOISE. You're very young, my son, you don't know anything about life, you haven't any experience. What would have become of you without me? Life has always been very easy for you. You're used to your mother giving you everything you want. You must remember what I say. I speak as a mother, and a mother lives only for her children. Respect your mother, respect her, if only for the white hairs which adorn her brow. Think that your mother does everything for you out of affection. When, my son, have you ever seen your mother do anything for herself? I have thought only of you. First my children, and then my husband. I don't count, not for anybody, and even less for myself. That is why, my son, now that I am going to take care of your father's wounds, you mustn't stand in my way. Others would kiss the ground I tread on. I don't ask so much from you, I merely hope that you may find it in you to thank me for my efforts. *(Pause.)*

Françoise goes towards the torture chamber with the salt and vinegar.

I'll go and put a little salt and vinegar on poor little Daddy's wounds.

Maurice seizes his mother's arm brutally and prevents her from going into the room.

BENOÎT. Don't hold Mother's arm!

FRANÇOISE. Let him hit me. It's what he's always wanted. Look at the marks of his fingers on my poor arm. That's what he's always wanted to do—hit me.

BENOÎT *(very angry)*. How dare you hit Mother?

Benoît tries to hit his brother. Françoise throws herself between her sons to stop them fighting.

FRANÇOISE. No, my son, not in my presence. The family is sacred. I don't want my sons to fight.

Benoît controls himself with difficulty.

He can flay me alive if he wants to, but *please,* my child, don't hit him in my presence. I don't want any quarrels between brothers in my presence. He has hit me; but I forgive him.

Loud cry from her husband.

He is suffering—they are making him suffer. . . . He's suffering a great deal. I must put some vinegar on him as quickly as possible. At once.

Françoise goes into the torture chamber.

VOICE OF FRANÇOISE. Just a little salt and vinegar will do you a lot of good. Don't move, I haven't got much. There, there we are.

Groan from Jean.

That's it, there, there, now a bit of salt.

Angry cry from Jean.

MAURICE *(shouts).* Daddy! *(and weeps).*

VOICE OF FRANÇOISE. That's it, just a tiny bit more, there, a tiny bit more, don't move. *(Françoise speaks in gasps).* Don't move. There. Just a bit more.

Groan from Jean.

That's it, just a bit more; there, there it'll do you good.

Cry from Jean.

Just to finish it up, there.

Cry from Jean.

VOICE OF FRANÇOISE. That's all I've got!

Long silence. Cry from Jean. Silence.

Well now, how are your sore places? I'll touch them to see how they are.

Loud cry from Jean. Maurice, when his brother isn't looking, goes into the room.

VOICE OF MAURICE. What are you doing? You're scratching his wounds!

Maurice pushes his mother out of the room. Benoît throws himself on to his brother, about to hit him. The mother comes between them and separates the brothers.

FRANÇOISE. No, my son, no. *(To Benoît.)* You're hurting *me,* not him! No, don't hit your brother. I don't want you to hit him.

Benoît calms down.

BENOÎT. I won't tolerate him hurting you.

FRANÇOISE. Yes, let him hurt me. Let him if he enjoys it. That's what he wants. Let him. He wants me to cry when he hits me. My son, that's how your brother's made. What a martyr! What a cross! Why, O God, have I deserved to have a son who doesn't love me and who is only waiting for me to have a moment of weakness to beat and torment me!

BENOÎT *(furious)*. Maurice!

FRANÇOISE. Gently, my son, gently. *(Dejected.)* What a cross! What a cross, O God! Why do you punish me thus, Lord? What have I done to provoke such a punishment? Don't fight, my children, for the sake of your poor mother who never ceases to suffer, for the sake of her white hairs. *(To Benoît.)* And if *he* won't take pity on my sufferings, you at least, Benoît, must have pity on me and not make me suffer.

Or can it be that you don't love me either? *(Benoît, moved, tries to say something. His mother doesn't let him speak, and continues.)* Yes, that's it, you don't love me either.

BENOÎT *(on the verge of tears)*. Yes Mother, *I* do—*I* love you.

FRANÇOISE. Well then, why do you add extra thorns to the crown of sorrows I bear?

BENOÎT. Mother!

FRANÇOISE. Don't you see my sorrow? Don't you see the boundless sorrow of a mother?

BENOÎT *(nearly crying)*. Yes.

FRANÇOISE. Thank you, my son, you are the support of my old age. You are the unique consolation that God has given me in this life.

The executioners can again be heard whipping Jean. The husband sobs. All three—Françoise and her sons, listen in silence.

FRANÇOISE. They're beating him again. . . . And they must be hurting him a lot. . . . *(Françoise speaks in gasps.)* He's crying! He's crying. . . . He's groaning, isn't he? *(No one answers.)* . . . Yes, yes, he's groaning, he's groaning, I can hear him perfectly. . . .

Sounds of the whip, and groans. Jean suddenly gives a more piercing cry. The executioners continue their blows. Jean doesn't groan any more. Françoise goes to the door and looks into the room.

They've killed him! They've killed him!

Absolute silence. Maurice sits down, puts his head on the table. He is crying, perhaps. Silence. Long pause. Enter the two executioners with Jean, tied up as before. Jean is dead. His head hangs down inertly.

FRANÇOISE *(to the executioners)*. Let me see him. Let me see him properly.

The executioners, without paying any attention to Françoise, cross the room and go out by the street door. Françoise and Benoît sit down on either side of Maurice. They look at him. Silence.

MAURICE *(To Françoise)*. They killed Daddy because of you.

FRANÇOISE. How dare you say that to your mother? To your mother who has always taken so much trouble with you.

MAURICE *(interrupting her)*. Don't give me all that stuff. What I'm accusing you of is of denouncing Daddy.

Benoît is too depressed to intervene.

FRANÇOISE. Yes, my son, as you wish. If it gives you any pleasure I'll say it was my fault. Is that what you want?

MAURICE. Oh, stop harping on that. *(Pause. Long silence.)* Why did you treat Daddy like that, Daddy who never gave you anything to complain of?

FRANÇOISE. That's it. That's what I've been waiting for, all my life. When your father compromised the future of his children and his wife because of his. . . .

MAURICE *(interrupting her)*. What's all that stuff about compromising the future? What's your latest invention?

FRANÇOISE. Ah, my son! What misery! What a cross! *(Pause.)* Of course he compromised his children's future by his failings. He knew very well that if he continued in his guilty ways he would sooner or later finish up the way he has. He knew it only too well, but he didn't change, he continued, whatever happened, on his guilty way. How many times did I tell him so! How many times did I tell him: you're going to leave me a widow and your sons orphans. But what did he do? He ignored my advice and persisted in the error of his ways.

MAURICE. You're the only one who says he was guilty.

FRANÇOISE. Ah yes, naturally, you're not content now with having insulted me all night long, but you're going to call me a liar as well and swear that I make people perjure themselves. That's the way you treat a mother who, ever since you were born, has given you all her care and attention. While your father was compromising your future with his misbehaviour, I was thinking of your happiness and I had only one aim—to make you happy, to give you all the happiness that I had never known. Because for me, the only thing that counts is that your brother and you should be all right, everything else was of no importance. I'm a poor, ignorant, uneducated woman, who wants nothing but the good of her children, whatever the cost.

BENOÎT *(conciliatingly)*. Maurice, there isn't any point in making a fuss now; Daddy's dead, we can't do anything about it now.

FRANÇOISE. Benoît's right.

Long silence.

MAURICE. We could have prevented Daddy's death.

FRANÇOISE. How? Was it my fault? No. He was the one who was guilty—he, your father. What could I do? What could I do to stop him being like that? He'd got stubborn. I'm only a poor, ignorant, uneducated woman, I've spent my whole life doing nothing but worrying about other people, forgetting myself. When have you seen me buy a pretty dress or go to the cinema or to first nights, which I used to like so much? No, I didn't do any of those things, in spite of all the pleasure I'd have got out of them, and that was only because I preferred to devote myself entirely to you. I only ask one thing— that you shouldn't be ungrateful, and that you should be capable of appreciating the sacrifice of a mother like the one you were lucky enough to have.

BENOÎT. Yes, Mother, *I* appreciate all you've done for us.

FRANÇOISE. Yes, I know *you* do, but your brother doesn't.
It doesn't seem anything to your brother, it isn't enough for
him. How happy we could be if only we were all united, if
only we all agreed!

BENOÎT. Maurice, yes, we ought to understand one another
and all three live in peace. Mother is very good, I know she
loves you very much and that she'll give you everything you
need. Even if it's only out of selfishness, come back to us. We'll
all three live happily and joyfully together and love one another.

MAURICE. But.... *(Pause.)* Daddy....

Silence.

BENOÎT. That's already past history. Don't look backwards.
What matters is the future. It would be too stupid to hang
on to the past. You'll have everything you want with mother.
Everything that's hers will be yours. Isn't that so, Mother?

FRANÇOISE. Yes, my son, everything that is mine will be
his; I forgive him.

BENOÎT. You see how good she is; she even forgives you.

FRANÇOISE. Yes, I forgive you, and I shall forget all your
insults.

BENOÎT. She'll forget everything! *(Gaily.)* That's the important thing. And so we'll all three live together without ill-
feeling; Mother, you and me. What could be more wonderful?

MAURICE *(half convinced)*. Yes, but....

BENOÎT *(interrupting him)*. No, you mustn't be vindictive.
Be like Mother. She has reason to be angry with you, but she's
promised to forget everything. We shall be happy if you'll be
nice.

*Maurice, full of emotion, lowers his head. Long silence.
Benoît puts his arm round his brother.*

Kiss Mother.

Silence.

Kiss her and let bygones be bygones.

Maurice goes up to his mother and kisses her.

FRANÇOISE. My son!

BENOÎT *(to Maurice)*. Ask Mother to forgive you.

MAURICE *(nearly crying)*. Forgive me, Mother.

Maurice and Françoise embrace. Benoît joins them and all three stay enfolded in each others' arms while the

Curtain falls

FANDO AND LIS

CHARACTERS

Lis, the woman in the pram
Fando, the man who is taking her to Tar
and the three men with the umbrella :
Namur
Mitaro
Toso

The Play is in five scenes.

Scene One

Fando and Lis are sitting on the ground. Near them is a large perambulator. It is old and black, its paint is peeling and it has thick rubber wheels with rusty spokes. Various objects are tied on to its sides with bits of string; among them are a drum, a rolled-up blanket, a fishing rod, a football and an earthenware casserole. Lis has both legs paralysed.

LIS. But I shall die and no one will remember me.

FANDO *(very affectionately)*. Yes, they will, Lis, I shall remember you, and I'll come and see you in the cemetery with a flower and a dog.

Long pause. Fando looks at Lis.

(with feeling). And at your funeral I'll sing very softly the old song: "What fun a funeral is, what fun a funeral is"; its music is so amusing. *(He looks at her silently and adds with a satisfied air.)* I'll do that for you.

LIS. You love me a lot.

FANDO. But I'd rather you didn't die. *(Pause.)* I shall be terribly sad the day you die.

LIS. Be terribly sad? Why?

FANDO *(disconsolate)*. I don't know.

LIS. You only say that because you've heard other people saying it. What it means is that you *won't* be sad. You're always deceiving me.

FANDO. No, Lis, I'm telling you the truth. I shall be very sad.

LIS. Will you cry?

FANDO. I'll do my best, but I don't know if I'll be able to.

LIS. I don't know if I'll be able to! I don't know if I'll be able to! D'you think that's any sort of answer?

FANDO. Believe me, Lis.

LIS. But believe what?

FANDO *(pondering)*. I don't really know; just tell me that you believe me.

LIS *(like an automaton)*. I believe you.

FANDO. That's no good; not when you say it like that.

LIS *(gaily)*. I believe you.

FANDO. It's no good like that, either. *(Humbly.)* Lis, when you want to, you know very well how to say things.

LIS *(in another tone of voice, equally insincere)*. I believe you.

FANDO *(discouraged)*. No, Lis, no. That's not it. Try again.

LIS *(makes an effort, but her words don't seem any more sincere than they did before)*. I believe you.

FANDO *(very sad)*. No, no, Lis. How nasty you are to me! Try again, but properly.

LIS *(without managing it)*. I believe you.

FANDO *(violently)*. No, no, that's not it.

LIS *(making a desperate effort)*. I believe you.

FANDO *(still more violently)*. Not like that, either!

LIS *(full of sincerity)*. I believe you.

FANDO *(moved)*. Lis! You believe me?

LIS *(also moved)*. Yes, I believe you.

FANDO. Oh, I'm so happy, Lis.

LIS. I believe you because when you talk you look like a rabbit, and when you sleep with me you let me take all the blankets and you catch cold.

FANDO. I don't mind.

LIS. And specially because in the mornings you wash me in the fountain, and then I don't have to do it myself, and I don't like doing it myself.

FANDO *(after a pause, with a very determined air)*. Lis, I want to do a lot of things for you.

LIS. How many?

FANDO *(thinking)*. As many as possible.

LIS. Then what you ought to do is to stand up for yourself in life.

FANDO. That's very difficult.

LIS. That's the only thing you can do for me.

FANDO. Stand up for myself? What will you come out with next! *(Pause.)* It almost sounds like a joke. *(Very seriously.)* But Lis, I don't know why I ought to stand up for myself, and perhaps if I did know I wouldn't be strong enough, and if I *were* strong enough I don't know if being strong would help me get the better of things.

LIS. Make an effort, Fando.

FANDO. Make an effort? *(Pause.)* Perhaps that'd be easier.

LIS. We really ought to agree.

FANDO. And are you sure that that would be any use to us?

LIS. Almost sure.

FANDO *(he's thinking)*. But be some use for what?

LIS. It doesn't matter much; what does matter is that it should be some use to us.

FANDO. Everything is so simple for you.

LIS. No, everything is very difficult for me too.

FANDO. But you find a solution for everything.

LIS. No, I never find any solutions. What happens is that when I say I've found one, I'm lying.

FANDO. But that's not fair.

LIS. I know it's not fair. But as no one ever asks me anything, it comes to the same thing. And anyway it makes a good impression.

FANDO. Yes, that's true, it makes a good impression. But what if someone does ask you something?

LIS. There's no danger. No one asks me anything.

FANDO. Oh, dear! Isn't it complicated!

LIS. Yes, very.

FANDO *(moved)*. You're so intelligent, Lis!

LIS. But it doesn't do me any good, you're always hurting me.

FANDO. No, no, I don't hurt you; it's very much the other way round.

LIS. Yes you do, just think how you beat me whenever you get a chance.

FANDO *(ashamed)*. It's true. I won't do it any more, you'll see.

LIS. You always say you won't do it any more, and then you torment me whenever you can, and you say you're going to chain me up so that I can't move. You make me cry.

FANDO *(very affectionate)*. I make you cry, and perhaps even just when you're having your period. No, Lis, I won't do it any more. *(Pause.)* I shall buy a boat when we get to Tar and I'll show you the river. Shall I, Lis?

LIS. Yes, Fando.

FANDO. And I shall feel all your pains, Lis, so that you can really see that I don't want to hurt you. *(Pause.)* I'll have children, like you, too.

LIS *(moved)*. Oh you are good!

FANDO. Would you like me to tell you some nice stories like the one about the man who was taking a paralysed woman to Tar in a little pram?

LIS. Carry me for a bit first.

FANDO. Yes, Lis. *(Fando takes Lis in his arms and carries her up and down the stage.)* Look, Lis, look how lovely the country is, and the road.

LIS. Yes. Oh, I am happy.

FANDO. Look at the flowers.

LIS. There aren't any flowers, Fando.

FANDO *(violently)*. That doesn't matter—look at the flowers.

LIS. I tell you there aren't any flowers.

D

Lis is now speaking in a very humble voice. Fando, on the contrary, becomes more and more dictatorial and brutal.

FANDO. I told you to look at the flowers! *(Shouting.)* Is it because you didn't understand what I said?

LIS. I did understand, Fando; forgive me. *(Long pause.)* How I regret being paralysed!

FANDO. It's a good thing you *are* paralysed, because I do the carrying.

Fando gets tired of carrying Lis; the more tired he gets the more violent he becomes.

LIS *(very gently, afraid of offending Fando)*. Isn't the country pretty, with its flowers and its lovely trees.

FANDO *(irritated)*. Where d'you see the trees?

LIS *(gently)*. That's what people say: the country with its lovely trees.

Pause.

FANDO. You're too heavy. *(Fando, without warning, lets Lis fall to the ground.)*

LIS *(with a cry of pain)*. Ow, Fando! *(Immediately gentle again, for fear of offending him.)* Oh, you did hurt me!

FANDO *(unkindly)*. Now you're going to start complaining again.

LIS *(on the verge of tears)*. No, I'm not complaining. Thank you very much, Fando. *(Pause.)* But I'd like it if you'd take me for a walk in the country and show me those lovely flowers.

Fando, visibly annoyed, takes Lis by one leg and drags her about the stage.

FANDO. Well, can you see them now, the flowers you wanted to see? Eh? Tell me. Well, have you seen enough?

LIS *(sobs, trying not to let Fando hear her. She is certainly suffering a great deal).* Yes . . . yes . . . thank you . . . Fando. . . .

FANDO. Where d'you want me to carry you to? To the pram?

LIS. Yes . . . if it isn't too much trouble.

Fando drags Lis by one hand towards the pram.

FANDO *(visibly annoyed).* I have to do everything for you, and you cry into the bargain.

LIS. Forgive me, Fando. *(She sobs.)*

FANDO. One fine day I shall abandon you and I shall go away, a long way away from you.

LIS *(crying).* No, Fando, don't abandon me. I haven't anyone else in the world but you.

FANDO. All you do is get in my way. *(Shouting.)* And don't cry!

LIS *(making an effort not to cry.)* I'm not crying.

FANDO. Don't cry, I tell you. If you cry I shall go away now.

Lis in spite of her efforts, continues to cry.

(very much annoyed). Well, so you're crying and all, eh? Well then I'm going right away and I shan't come back again.

Fando goes out, furious; after a few moments he comes in again on all fours and goes towards Lis.

(humbly). Forgive me, Lis.

Fando takes Lis in his arms and kisses her. Then he sits her down comfortably. She lets him do so without a word.

I won't be nasty to you any more.

LIS. Oh, you are good, Fando!

FANDO. Yes, Lis. You'll see how nice I'll be from now on.

LIS. Yes, Fando.

FANDO. Tell me what you'd like.

LIS. Us to start for Tar.

FANDO. We'll leave straightaway. *(He very carefully takes Lis in his arms and puts her in the pram.)* But we've been trying for a long time to get to Tar and we've never succeeded.

LIS. We'll try once more.

FANDO. All right, Lis, just as you like.

Fando pushes the pram, which slowly starts to cross the stage. Lis, from inside it, looks towards the back of the stage. Fando suddenly stops, goes towards Lis and strokes her face with both his hands. Pause.

I'm sorry about what happened. I didn't mean to make you unhappy.

LIS. I know you didn't, Fando.

FANDO. Have confidence in me, I won't do it any more.

LIS. Yes, I have confidence in you. You're always very good to me. I remember you sent me some very big letters when I was in hospital so's I could boast of getting very big letters.

FANDO *(flattered)*. Oh, that was nothing, Lis.

LIS. And I remember, too, that often, when you didn't have anything to say, you used to send me lots of toilet paper so that the letter would be bulky.

FANDO. That was nothing.

LIS. I was so happy!

FANDO. You see—you ought to trust me.

LIS. Yes, Fando, I *do* trust you. (*The pram goes off, pushed by Fando.*)

Curtain

Scene Two

The same place. Dusk.
Fando enters, pushing the pram with Lis in it. He stops. Slowly, and with great care, he lifts Lis out of the pram and puts her on the ground. A huge iron chain fastens one of Lis's feet to the pram. Fando now speaks in a softly despairing tone.

FANDO. Lis, I'm very tired. I'm going to have a rest for a moment.

Lis looks at him listlessly.

I say I'm very tired, and I'm going to sit down for a moment.

Lis looks at him without expression, and nods her head.

Do you want anything? Tell me if you want anything.

Lis doesn't answer.

Speak to me, Lis, say something, tell me something. I know what the matter is, you're cross with me because we aren't a single step farther on even though we've been walking for such a long time, and we're back where we started from.

It looks as if Lis hasn't heard any of this.

Lis, answer me. *(Imploring her.)* Do you want anything?
Speak to me, Lis.

Fando is still speaking in an imploring, pitiable tone.

Do you want me to move you? Aren't you comfortable like
that?

*Lis doesn't answer. Lis doesn't show the slightest interest in
Fando.*

I know what it is. You want me to move you.

*Fando moves her with great care. She lets him do so. He
is very attentive.*

There, you'll be more comfortable like that.

*Fando puts his hands on Lis's cheeks and looks at her en-
thusiastically.*

How pretty you are, Lis.

Fando kisses her. Lis still doesn't move.

Do say something, Lis. Talk to me. Are you bored? Would
you like me to play the drum for you? *(Fando looks at Lis,
waiting for an answer, then he adds, happily.)* Yes, I think
that's what it is, you want me to play the drum.

*Fando, now quite happy, goes over to the pram, unfastens
the drum, and puts it on a level with his stomach.*

What would you like me to play you?

Lis doesn't answer. Silence.

Right, I'll play you the feather tune. Would you like that?
(Silence.) Or would you rather I played the feather tune?

Silence. Lis doesn't answer.

Just as you like.

He is about to start playing the drum, but he stops short.

I feel a bit nervous, Lis. *(Silence.)* Right, I'll make an effort for you and I'll play you the feather song that you like so much.

He is about to start, but he can't bring himself to.

(ashamed). I'm sorry, but I don't know the feather song.

Pause. Suddenly Fando starts playing the drum rather clumsily, at the same time singing in a rather tuneless voice the following song.

The feather was in the bed
And the bed was in the feather,
The feather was in the bed
And the bed was in the feather.

When he has finished, he says to Lis.

Did you like it, Lis?

Lis doesn't say anything. Fando, much saddened, goes over to the pram to put the drum back. Before he puts it down he looks at Lis, suddenly grabs the drum and plays again. He looks sideways at Lis, but sees that she is indifferent to his music. He is discouraged, and abandons the drum near the pram.

(sadder than ever). Speak to me, Lis, speak to me, say something to me. How can we continue our journey if you don't speak to me? I'm getting tired. I feel I'm all alone. Speak to me, Lis, say something to me, tell me something, it doesn't matter what, even if it isn't nice, or if it's silly, but tell me something. You know how to talk very well when you want to. Don't forget me, Lis. *(Pause.)* Every so often you become silent and I don't know what's the matter with you. I don't

know if you're hungry or if you want some flowers or if you
feel like having a pee. Of course I might be wrong, I know
you don't owe me anything and that you might even be cross
with me, but that's no reason not to talk to me. *(Pause.)* I
got you the pram and I push you in it because I know you
want to go to Tar. The difficulties don't matter a bit, I only
want to do what you like best. *(Pause.)* But speak to me, Lis.

*Lis looks at him expressionlessly. Enter three men : Mitaro,
Namur and Toso. Namur walks with his two friends on
either side of him and carries a big black umbrella which
shelters all three of them. They form a single unit. They stop
a long way from Lis and Fando to inspect the surroundings,
and don't pay the slightest attention to them. After their
inspection, which in the case of Mitaro and Namur, who go
so far as to smell the ground, is particularly detailed, they
all three join up again under the umbrella.*

TOSO. Yes, it'll be all right to sleep here.

MITARO. But we have to find out which way the wind's
coming from, first. *(He wets his finger and holds it up in the
air.)*

NAMUR. That's not important. What matters is to know
which way it's going.

TOSO. Let's lie down under the umbrella and go to sleep,
and let's not bother with all that stuff about the wind.

MITARO *(hurt)*. You're still just as thoughtless as ever.

NAMUR. If we listened to him we'd all be dead by now.

MITARO. Dead or even worse, because of his filthy habit of
never taking any precautions.

TOSO *(obstinately)*. I think that what matters is to go to
sleep.

MITARO. What matters is to know which way the wind's coming from.

NAMUR *(gently admonishing him)*. No, what matters is to know which way it's going.

MITARO. I continue to assert that what matters is to know which way the wind's coming from.

NAMUR. Oh well, I don't want to appear uncompromising, I don't want to be like Toso. As you wish.

MITARO *(quite satisfied)*. Well then, let's say that what matters is to know which way the wind's coming from.

NAMUR *(conciliating)*. That's it, to know which way the wind's coming from. *(After a short pause, he adds more softly.)* And which way it goes after it's come.

TOSO *(interrupting him)*. So far as I'm concerned you can say what you like; it seems to me that what's really important is to go to sleep as soon as possible.

MITARO *(very angry)*. That's it, nothing could be easier; we go to sleep, and then what?

NAMUR. Yes, yes; and then what?

TOSO. And then . . . we'll see.

MITARO. We'll see! That's how the worst catastrophes come about, from lack of foresight, because people haven't taken the slightest precaution.

NAMUR. Exactly, exactly. After all, how long would we need to take precautions? In actual fact, one minute. What risks should we avoid because of them? A very great number.

MITARO. Very well said.

TOSO. But I get tired when I take precautions.

MITARO. His lordship gets tired !

TOSO. And anyway, it's very difficult.

MITARO. Now he's going to discover that he can't make the smallest effort.

TOSO. It isn't a small effort, but a very big one.

MITARO. It'd give his lordship a hernia !

NAMUR. He may be right, the effort needed to foresee things is very great and very complicated. And it's becoming almost impossible to take the necessary precautions.

MITARO. Yes, I defer to the evidence. It's a great effort, but a momentary one, an effort that doesn't last long.

NAMUR. That doesn't last long? That depends on how you see it.

MITARO. Don't give me all that stuff again, I remember perfectly what you were telling me the other day, about how two phenomena which are simultaneous for an observer on the earth aren't simultaneous for an observer on a planet. From which you deduced that simultaneity is relative and that consequently time is also relative. And I told you that I personally didn't believe it, any more than I believe in Father Christmas.

NAMUR. Well, the only point I want to make is that the effort *doesn't* only last a short time.

MITARO *(angry, and not knowing what to answer, says nothing, but then says)*. But we've wandered from the point —which was to find out which way the wind's coming from.

NAMUR. Yes, so it was, we were trying to find out which way the wind's coming from . . . *(He adds, more softly)* in order to find out which way it's going.

MITARO. We were quite simply occupied with taking precautions to enable us to sleep in peace—and at once—when Toso said that the thing that mattered was to go to sleep.

TOSO. But. . . .

NAMUR *(interrupting him indignantly)*. Toso, you might just as well admit that so far you've stopped us sleeping, with all your nonsense and your lack of solidarity with our position.

Toso doesn't say anything.

MITARO. Not for a single moment did you stop to consider our position intelligently but, on the contrary, you dissociated yourself from our point of view in an ill-considered and destructive way.

TOSO. I simply said that what mattered was to go to sleep under the umbrella as quickly as possible.

NAMUR *(indignant)*. What a nerve! And you still dare to proclaim it cynically without begging our pardon. If I were you the blush of shame would rise to my face. And here we are, still arguing, and all because of you.

MITARO. Yes, because of you and no one else.

NAMUR. As you saw, I abandoned my first position, which maintained that the important thing was to find out which way the wind is coming from, in favour of a speedier agreement which would facilitate a short installation and this, be it said in passing, when it's as plain as the nose on your face that what really matters is to know which way the wind is going.

MITARO *(smiling, but incisive)*. Without any too great a wish to contradict you, I should like it to be clearly established that what matters is to find out which way the wind is coming from.

NAMUR *(trying to smile to hide his anger)*. I take the liberty of adding that everyone will agree to recognise the fact that what matters is to find out which way the wind's going.

Fando, who has followed the conversation of the men with the umbrella, is very much interested, and goes over to them.

FANDO *(bashfully)*. I beg your pardon. Excuse me. It was so nice listening to your argument from over there. *(He points to the place where he was before.)* How well you do it! Will you let me argue too?

The three men with the umbrella look at each other, most annoyed.

Let me argue with you. *(Pause.)* She doesn't want to talk to me and there are lots of things I'd so like to tell someone. I'm all by myself.

The three men with the umbrella, very angry, lie down on the ground under the umbrella and start to go to sleep.

(humbly). There are lots of things I can do. I can help you if you'll talk to me. *(Pause. He continues, a bit bashfully)* I can play the drum, too. *(He laughs shyly)* Not very well, but I know some nice songs like the feather song. You're going to hear something good now.

Fando goes to fetch his drum. The men with the umbrella are sleeping conscientiously; one of them is snoring.

(While he's putting the drum where he wants it) I'll play and sing for you, but only on the express condition that you talk to me. *(He moves over towards them.)* Don't you hear me? *(Fando notices that they are asleep. He goes back sadly to Lis.)* They didn't take any notice of me, Lis. I've got lots of things to say to them and I was even going to sing them the feather song.

Silence. Lis continues not to see him.

(to Lis, gently). You're better than they are, Lis. You can say all sorts of nice things. Speak to me.

Lis is silent. Long silence.

D'you want me to put on a show for your benefit? I'll do some acrobatics, shall I?

Lis is silent. Fando executes a series of exercises which are a mixture of ballet, of a clown's antics and of the movements of a drunkard. Finally, standing on one leg, he brings the knee of the other one up to meet his elbow, while he pulls long noses with the hand of the same arm, and at the same time utters cries of joy.

FANDO. Look how difficult it is, Lis. Look how difficult it is.

Lis is silent. Fando finishes his number dejectedly and in silence. He goes over to Lis and wanders round her very sadly. Silence.

(in a plaintive voice, not shouting). Speak to me, Lis. Speak to me.

Curtain

Scene Three

Same place. The men with the umbrella (Namur, Mitaro and Toso) are talking to Fando. Lis seated in her pram, is a few yards away from them.

NAMUR. It's many years since we decided to do it.

FANDO. I've heard that it's impossible to get there.

NAMUR. No, it isn't that it's impossible. Quite simply, no one ever *has* got there, and no one ever thinks of getting there.

MITARO. But *trying* to isn't so complicated.

FANDO. Shan't we ever get there, she and I, then?

MITARO. Your conditions are better than ours. You have a pram. That makes the journey easier and quicker for you.

FANDO. Yes, of course, I'm quicker, but I always come back to the same place.

MITARO. The same thing happens to us; it's quite useless for us to set out on the way to Tar, we always come back to the same place.

MANUR. But that isn't the most serious drawback we're up against; the worst thing, probably, is that we don't take any precautions.

MITARO. Yes, Namur's right, that's the worst thing. We'd have been so much further on if we'd taken some precautions.

TOSO *(annoyed)*. Oh, there you go again with your precautions. I've already told you that what matters is to continue our journey.

NAMUR *(disconsolate)*. To tell the truth, it's Toso that stops us getting to Tar, Toso with his usual spirit of contradiction, his usual refusal to fit in with our way of seeing things.

MITARO. It isn't that we, Namur and I, think the same thing, or that we have the same ideas, but in the long run we come to an agreement, but he. . . . It's his fault we haven't got to Tar yet. Yesterday, not to go any further back. . . .

NAMUR *(cutting him short)*. Yes, the business about the wind, and wanting to go to sleep.

MITARO. Yes, that was it, that was it.

FANDO *(remembering enthusiastically)* Oh, you were arguing so well, it made such a good impression !

NAMUR *(ironically)*. Ah yes, a good impression. . . .

MITARO. Didn't you hear what we were saying ?

FANDO. Yes, I did, but I didn't pay any attention to it, I only heard the music. It was nice music. *(Humming)* Tralalee, tralala, dohrayme, meraydoh, taratoh, taratah.

NAMUR. That's true. It must have been nice.

FANDO. It sounded lovely from over there.

MITARO. That's the trouble; it's fine when you hear it from a distance, it's musical, but what happens ?

NAMUR. The worst, the very worst.

MITARO. We can't prevent him sowing discord in our union. He's a pig, there's no doubt about it.

NAMUR. Even worse than a pig.

Fando is thinking. Silence.

FANDO *(intervening)*. What was it you asked? What's worse than a pig ? Or what's better than a pig ?

NAMUR. I don't know, it'll probably turn out that this chap knows all about animals.

FANDO. No, I'm simply asking whether what he's trying to think of *(he points to Mitaro)* is animals which are better or worse than pigs.

MITARO *(after a long pause)*. I've forgotten.

NAMUR *(reproaching him)*. Still just as forgetful and just as philanthropic.

MITARO *(annoyed)*. You see how you're always trying to insult me. *(He ponders.)* Just to show you, just to rile you, I remember perfectly well what I asked you, and that was: which are the animals that are worse than pigs and which are the ones that are better.

FANDO *(terribly pleased, his words coming out with a rush)*. I know. The worse ones are the lion, the cockroach, the goat and the cat, and the better ones are the cow, the hare, the sheep, the parrot and the kangaroo.

NAMUR. The kangaroo?

FANDO. Yes, the kangaroo.

NAMUR. Did you say the kangaroo is worse?

FANDO *(a little bashfully)*. Yes, yes.

NAMUR. But are you sure?

FANDO *(hesitantly)*. ... Yes.

NAMUR. But ... sure, *sure*?

FANDO *(in tears)*. You're too much for me.

MITARO *(to Namur, reproachfully)*. You've made him cry.

NAMUR. Yes, but the fellow isn't sure of anything, and he indulges in positive statements which, good God....

MITARO. But you made him cry as if he were a man going to Tar with a woman in a pram.

FANDO *(excusing him)*. But I only cried a very little—two drops.

TOSO *(obstinately)*. I think what we ought to do is argue less and try and get to Tar.

MITARO *(satisfied and hurt)*. You see how he is—he's always like that. When we're just about to leave, when we're on the point of coming to an agreement, then he comes out with some idiocy.

NAMUR. He's unbearable.

FANDO. Then why do you let him be with you?

NAMUR. It would take a very long time to tell you that.

MITARO. An eternity.

TOSO *(inflexibly)*. We should stop all this discussion and start off for Tar.

MITARO *(reprimanding Toso)*. Is that how you help us? We try to bring our discussion with this man to an end so that we can start off for Tar, and what do you do? You pester us, you annoy us day and night.

NAMUR. You're so negative and so unsociable.

MITARO *(to Fando)*. You see, it's really a pity. Don't you think so?

FANDO. Yes, I do indeed.

Silence.

MITARO. But you—you're really happy with her.

FANDO. Yes, of course; she doesn't bother me in the least. She's charming.

MITARO. What luck!

FANDO. Come and see her.

Mitaro and Namur go and see Lis with Fando. Her eyes are wide open but she looks as if she's miles away and lets Fando touch her without making the slightest movement.

(enthusiastically). Look at her.

Fando takes Lis's head and turns it in various directions, saying.

Look how beautiful she is.

MITARO. Yes, she's very beautiful.

FANDO. Bend down, so that you can see her better from underneath, in perspective.

Mitaro and Namur, squatting, look at Lis. Fando continues to place her in different positions.

FANDO. Come over here, you'll see how pretty she is.

The two men go over to the pram.

Look at her pretty legs, look how soft the material of her slip is.

Mitaro and Namur touch her slip.

MITARO. It's true, it's very soft.

FANDO *(really pleased).* Look how white and soft her thighs are.

Fando lifts up Lis's slip so that the men can see her thighs.

MITARO. It's true, they're white and soft.

Fando rearranges her slip with great care.

FANDO. What I like best is kissing her. Her face is very soft, it's a pleasure to stroke it. Stroke it.

MITARO. Now, this minute?

FANDO. Yes, stroke it like this.

Fando takes Lis's face in his two hands and lets them slide down her face tenderly.

Go on, stroke her, you'll see how nice it is.

Mitaro strokes Lis's face with one hand.

No, use both hands.

Mitaro strokes her very respectfully.

Well, what d'you think of her?

MITARO *(enthusiastically)*. Very nice.

FANDO. You too. *(He points to Namur.)*

Namur strokes her.

FANDO. Kiss her, too, like I do.

Fando kisses Lis rapidly on the mouth.

Go on, you'll see how nice it is.

Namur and Mitaro kiss Lis on the lips, very respectfully. Lis is still expressionless.

Well? Did you like it?

NAMUR. ⎫
MITARO. ⎬ Yes, very much.

FANDO *(very pleased)*. Well, she's my fiancée.

MITARO. For always?

FANDO. Yes, for always.

MITARO. And don't you ever get tired of her?

TOSO *(interrupting him)*. When are we going to start for Tar?

MITARO *(after a short pause)*. You see what he's like?

FANDO. Yes.

NAMUR. He never lets us finish.

TOSO. What *I* say is, we ought to get started for Tar as soon as possible.

MITARO *(indulgently)*. Excuse all his faux pas. He's just like that. He was born like that, there's nothing to be done to cure him.

NAMUR. You can't teach him anything, it's useless. The moment we're going to do something he immediately comes and disturbs us with his complications. He never lets us come to an agreement.

FANDO. But he may be right in saying that it would be a good thing to get started.

NAMUR. "Right", what might be called "right"—he always is to some extent.

MITARO. I must say that what he says isn't entirely off the point.

NAMUR. That's true; when you come to think about it he is sometimes just a tiny bit right. Not very right, naturally, but just a bit.

MITARO. That may be the very thing that holds us back. What I mean is, we always find that there's *some* sense underlying everything he says, even if it's a long way down.

NAMUR. A very long way down.

MITARO. Yes, yes, a very long way down, but at least we find that there is *something* underlying it. That's why, even though we consider his ideas absurd and destructive, we always accept them; we discuss them and even try and get him to see the good and bad sides of them.

TOSO. Personally, what I think is, we ought to start off for Tar.

NAMUR *(very pleased)*. You see?

MITARO *(pleased too)*. You understand?

FANDO. Yes, yes, I see.

MITARO. And it would be so easy for him to keep quiet.

FANDO. Is it easy to keep quiet?

MITARO. I don't say that one shouldn't take all the necessary precautions, nor even that one shouldn't have some experience, but in reality if you really try you can manage to keep quiet.

FANDO. Well, I did try one day . . . and you needn't think it was plain sailing.

NAMUR. Ah! What an interesting man! What a lot of things he's done!

MITARO. And what happened to you when you tried?

FANDO *(blushing)*. It was amusing.

MITARO. Tell us, tell us. Oh, how interesting!

NAMUR. What happened? What did you do?

FANDO. I got up in the morning and I said to myself: "To-day I'm not going to say a word all day."

NAMUR *(trying to understand, repeats out loud)*. He got up in the morning and he said to himself: "Today I'm not going to say a word all day."

FANDO *(continuing)*. And then. . . .

NAMUR *(interrupting again)*. There's something I don't quite understand: you told us that you were trying not to say anything all day—then how did you talk to yourself?

MITARO. Don't be an idiot: he talked to himself mentally.

NAMUR. Ah! That changes everything.

MITARO. Go on, go on, I'm very interested.

FANDO. Well then, having decided not to speak, I started to wonder what I could do to offset the silence, and I began to walk up and down.

NAMUR. You must have felt very pleased.

FANDO. I did at first, I walked like mad. But the worst was to come.

Fando is silent.

NAMUR *(very much interested)*. What happened?

MITARO. Tell us, tell us.

FANDO. No, I can't tell you. It's too private.

NAMUR. Are you really going to leave us like that, all agog?

FANDO. It's better if I leave it at that—the story ends unhappily.

NAMUR. Really unhappily?

FANDO *(on the verge of tears)*. Yes, yes, very unhappily.

NAMUR. What a pity!

MITARO. Isn't it! How sad!

TOSO. It'd be best if we started for Tar.

Silence and consternation.

MITARO. You see? Why insist?

FANDO. Yes, yes, quite so.

MITARO. That's what I like most about you. You understand us. Because, sometimes, people don't even understand us. The other day we met someone else who was also going to Tar and who insisted on saying he was right all the time.

FANDO. I saw at once that it was you who were right and not he. The moment you started talking about the wind I understood that.

MITARO. And how was it you understood so quickly?

FANDO. It's easy for me. I said to myself. . . .

NAMUR *(interrupting him)*. Mentally?

MITARO. Of course, my dear fellow!

NAMUR *(astonished)*. What a chap! The way he talks to himself mentally!

FANDO. Well then, I said to myself: the first one who says "which way" will be right, and as you said it before he did I knew that he wasn't right.

NAMUR *(enthusiastically)*. That's a good way of finding out who's right.

FANDO. Yes, it's an excellent way.

NAMUR. And do you always use it?

FANDO. Nearly always.

MITARO. You must have had a lot of experience.

FANDO. Yes, quite a bit. Although I use other methods sometimes.

NAMUR *(he couldn't be more astonished)*. Other methods?

FANDO *(flattered)*. Yes, of course.

NAMUR. What a tremendously inventive chap!

MITARO. All that trouble to find out where the Right is!

FANDO. I've used various infallible systems to discover it ever since I was a child.

NAMUR. That's what we should have done, and not wasted our time the way we have wasted it.

MITARO. This isn't the moment to be sorry for ourselves.

NAMUR *(annoyed)*. No, of course it's not. *(Pause.) And* what other systems have you used to discover who's in the right?

FANDO. I've used one which had to do with the days of the week, but it's very complicated.

MITARO *(interested)*. What sort of system is that?

FANDO. It's like this: on the days which are multiples of three, men who wear glasses are in the right. On even days, mothers are in the right, and on the days which end in a nought, nobody's right.

MITARO *(enthusiastically)*. Oh, that's good!

FANDO. But it's very complicated: you have to be sure what day it is and not make a mistake—that's how I've sometimes said that someone was right when he was wrong.

MITARO *(alarmed)*. That's bad!

FANDO. Very bad! It often used to stop my nails growing.

MITARO. I can understand why you prefer your present method.

FANDO. It's simpler, when you come to think of it.

NAMUR. Simpler? And what if no one says the words "which way"?

FANDO. I've thought of everything. If after five minutes no one has said the words "which way", I say that the first person to say the word "fly" is right.

MITARO *(astonished)*. Very comprehensive.

FANDO *(complacently)*. Yes, yes, there's no doubt about it. It's a very comprehensive system.

NAMUR. And what if no one says the word "fly"?

FANDO. Well then, I substitute the word "tree".

MITARO *(amazed)*. What foresight!

FANDO *(flattered)*. Yes, I mustn't grumble.

NAMUR. And what if no one says the word "tree"?

FANDO. Then I say that the first person to say the word "water" is right.

MITARO *(completely dumbfounded)*. Good God! Fancy anticipating all that!

FANDO *(very complacent)*. I always prefer to do something completely. In the long run it makes you feel better, even though it's more trouble at first.

NAMUR *(odiously)*. And what if no one says the word "water"?

Fando and Mitaro look at Namur with hostility. Silence. Namur is ashamed of himself.

I'm only asking what happens if no one says the word "water". I'm not trying to insult him.

MITARO *(embarrassed)*. It's not only an insult, but it looks as if you've got something against him, as well.

NAMUR *(bewildered)*. All right, all right, I didn't ask a thing.

MITARO. That's better.

NAMUR *(under his breath)*. Though I know very well that if no one says the word "water" the whole system collapses.

MITARO *(indignant)*. You're as pig-headed as Toso.

FANDO. It doesn't really matter, because I've thought of that one too. If no one says the word "water", I say that the first person to say . . . *(he hesitates)* to say . . . *(he ponders)* to say . . . the word . . . the word . . . "word", is right.

NAMUR. That's cheating, you've only just thought it up.

MITARO. You make me ashamed of you, Namur, you're always putting your foot in it.

FANDO. No, it isn't at all certain, I haven't just thought it up.

NAMUR. Well, tell us then, when did you try it out?

FANDO *(embarrassed)*. To tell you the truth, I haven't tried it out yet.

NAMUR *(to Mitaro)*. You see, you see.

TOSO *(interrupting him)*. When are we going to get started for Tar?

Silence. The three look at one another, impressed by Toso's question.

MITARO. We really *should* get started.

FANDO. Are you going to let me come with you?

NAMUR. With us?

FANDO. Yes, with you.

NAMUR. I don't know. We'll have to find out whether we're all three in agreement. *(To Mitaro.)* What's *your* opinion?

MITARO. Well—let him come.

NAMUR *(talking more or less in Mitaro's ear so that Fando shan't hear)*. But you must take into account the fact that he'll be bringing a woman and a pram. We can't allow ourselves the luxury of such company. It's too much of a responsibility.

MITARO. But what does it matter?

NAMUR *(almost black in the face)*. Be careful, he'll hear us. *(Fando starts whistling so that they can see that he's not listening.)* Have you really considered everything that can happen to us? Just think : no more and no less than a woman and a pram. Do you realise the responsibility that would weigh us down? Do you realise the number of precautions we should have to take?

MITARO. Yes, of course I do. So what? It doesn't make any difference.

NAMUR *(still speaking in Mitaro's ear)*. Doesn't make any difference . . . doesn't make any difference. . . . That's so easy to say! Don't come and tell me afterwards that I didn't warn you. *(Aloud, so that Fando can hear, with visible bad temper in spite of his forced smile)*. Good, well then you, Mitaro, are in favour of his coming with us?

MITARO *(embarrassed)*. How many times do I have to say so?

NAMUR. Good, good. *(To Toso.)* And you, Toso?

TOSO. Personally, all I want is for us to get going once and for all, and it's all the same to me whether it's with this man or without him.

NAMUR *(annoyed, but smiling)*. So we're all agreed—you can come with us.

FANDO. Oh, good!

MITARO. Then we'll get going.

The three men huddle together under the umbrella. Fando installs Lis comfortably in the pram.

FANDO. And when shall we arrive?

NAMUR. Oh, no one knows anything about that.

FANDO. I've heard it said that nobody has ever arrived, even though almost everybody has tried.

NAMUR. Old wives' tales.

The three men under the umbrella start walking off. Fando follows them, pushing the pram with Lis in it. They all go out slowly.

Curtain

Scene Four

Same place. Fando comes in, pushing the pram, with Lis in it. Fando stops.

FANDO. What's the matter with you?

LIS. I'm ill.

FANDO. What d'you want me to do, Lis?

LIS. Take me out of the pram.

Fando picks Lis up with great care and takes her out of the pram. Lis still has a long iron chain round her ankle which is fastened to the pram.

FANDO. Where does it hurt?

LIS. I don't know.

FANDO. That's the trouble! If I knew what illness you had, everything would be different.

LIS. But I feel very ill.

FANDO *(very sadly)*. Don't die, will you.

LIS. I know something's wrong with me. I feel ill, Fando.

FANDO. What a pity the men with the umbrella aren't here. They know a lot of things, they'd certainly cure you.

LIS. But they must still be a long way off; you were walking very quickly.

FANDO. Yes, I've got a good start on them. *(Complacently.)* And yet we started at the same time—but I've got the pram.

LIS. Here we are once again at the same place. We haven't advanced at all.

FANDO. What a pessimist you are. The thing that counts is that we're in advance of them.

LIS. You ran, you went very fast. The speed didn't do me any good, I've told you that before.

FANDO *(ashamed)*. It's true; forgive me, Lis.

LIS. You always ask me to forgive you, but you never listen to me.

FANDO. It's true; I really am unkind to you. *(Pause.)*

LIS. And then you always say you're going to handcuff me, as if the chain wasn't enough.

FANDO. No, I won't handcuff you.

Pause.

LIS. You never listen to me; don't you remember that sometimes, when I wasn't paralysed, you used to tie me up to the bed and beat me with a strap.

FANDO. I didn't think it bothered you.

Lis. But I used to tell you. How many times did I tell you that I couldn't bear the pain.

Fando. Forgive me, Lis. I won't ever tie you up to the bed again and beat you with the strap. I promise I won't.

Lis. And afterwards you insisted on putting this chain on me so that I can't move away from the pram. I can hardly crawl.

Fando. That's true, Lis. You ought to have told me.

Lis. I'm always telling you, but you never listen to me.

Fando. Lis, don't talk seriously when I'm here; kiss me.

Lis *(adopting a resigned air)*. You think that makes everything all right again.

Fando. You're tormenting me, Lis. *(Depressed. Silence. He continues, delighted.)* Who'm I going to give a little kiss-kiss to, on her mouth?

Lis. Don't make jokes, Fando.

Fando. Don't be cross with me, Lis; I *know* I'm to blame but don't be cross with me, you'll make me very sad.

Lis. You needn't think that makes everything all right.

Fando. Kiss me, Lis. *(Lis, very serious and expressionless, lets Fando kiss her passionately.)* Forget all about it, and don't make me think about all these things any more.

Silence.

Lis. Yesterday you insisted on leaving me naked on the road all night, and that's certainly why I'm ill.

Fando. But I did it so that all the men who came by could see you . . . so that everyone could see how pretty you are.

Lis. It was terribly cold, I was shivering.

FANDO. Poor Lis. . . . But the men looked at you and felt very happy, and they must certainly have gone on their way more gaily.

LIS. But I felt terribly alone and I was terribly cold.

FANDO. I was by your side. Didn't you see me? And lots of men stroked you when I asked them to. *(Pause.)* But I won't do it any more, Lis, I can see you don't like it.

LIS. You always say that.

FANDO. The thing is, you're funny sometimes, and you don't realise that everything I do is for your good. *(Pause. He is remembering.)* You were very pretty, naked. It was a marvellous sight.

LIS. It's never so funny for me.

FANDO. No, Lis. What a pity you don't see yourself with my eyes.

LIS. Fando, I'm so ill, I feel so ill.

FANDO. What d'you want me to do for you, Lis?

LIS. There's nothing to be done now. *(Pause.)* What I'd like is for you always to treat me well.

FANDO. Yes, Lis; I'll treat you well.

LIS. But make an effort.

FANDO. Right, that's what I'll do.

Pause. Lis notices a bulge in Fando's pocket.

LIS. But what have you got in your pocket?

Fando, like a child caught in the act of doing something silly, tries to hide it.

FANDO. Something.

Lis. Tell me what it is.

Fando. No, no.

Lis *(authoritatively)*. Show me what you're hiding.

Fando. It's nothing wrong.

Lis. Show it to me, I tell you.

Fando pathetically brings a pair of iron handcuffs out of his pocket.

You see : handcuffs.

Fando. But I'm not going to do anything wrong with them, they're just to play with.

Lis. You see, you're only waiting till I'm off my guard for a moment and then you'll put them on me.

Fando. No, Lis, I won't put them on you.

Lis. Throw them away, then.

Fando *(aggressively)*. No! *(He puts them back in his pocket.)*

Lis *(almost in tears)*. You see how you treat me.

Fando *(very much moved)*. Lis, don't cry. Lis, I love you very much. Don't cry, Lis.

Lis hugs him passionately.

Lis. Don't leave me, Fando, I haven't anyone but you. Don't treat me so badly.

Fando *(touched)*. How unkind I am to you! You'll see how nice I'll be now.

Lis. Take me in your arms, Fando, take me in your arms.

They embrace passionately.

I feel very ill.

FANDO. You'll soon be better and then we'll start off for Tar and we'll be very happy and I'll give you all the animals you see on the ground to play with—the cockroaches, the colorado beetles, the butterflies, the little ants, the toads . . . we'll sing together and I'll play the drum for you every day.

LIS. Yes, Fando, we'll be very happy.

FANDO. And we'll continue on our way to Tar.

LIS. That's right, to Tar.

FANDO. Yes, yes, both of us together.

Pause. They look at each other.

And when we get to Tar, you'll see how happy we shall be.

LIS. You're so good, Fando, and you're so kind to me.

FANDO. Yes, Lis, I'll do absolutely anything for you because I love you very much.

Fando goes over to the pram and undoes the drum with great care. Then, very deferentially, he shows it to Lis.

Look at the drum, Lis.

LIS. Isn't it pretty.

FANDO. Look how round it is.

LIS. Yes, so it is, it's quite round.

FANDO. Well, the only reason I have it is to be able to sing songs for you.

LIS. You're so good.

FANDO. When we get to Tar, we shall be so happy that I shall make up some new songs for you.

LIS. The feather song is very nice.

FANDO *(flattered)*. Pooh, that's nothing. I'll make up some much nicer ones. Other ones in which I won't only talk about feathers but *(he considers)* about birds' feathers as well, and . . . about eagles' feathers as well, and *(he considers, but can't think of anything)* and. . . .

LIS. And about feather markets as well.

FANDO *(pleased)*. Yes, yes, and about feather markets as well, and also about . . . about . . . about, er, and about feathers as well.

LIS. What lovely songs.

FANDO. I'll do all that for you.

LIS. You'll do it for me?

FANDO. Yes, Lis.

LIS. How good you are, Fando.

Pause. Fando suddenly takes out the handcuffs and looks at them nervously.

LIS *(gently)*. Don't hurt me.

FANDO *(very harshly)*. Why do you think I'm going to hurt you?

LIS *(gently)*. Don't talk to me like that, Fando.

FANDO *(very angry, he gets up and replies)*. I always talk to you in the same way.

LIS. What are you trying to do?

FANDO *(violently)*. Nothing.

LIS. Yes you are, you're trying to do something nasty. You know you are.

FANDO *(violently)*. There you go again.

LIS *(humbly)*. I can see you want to handcuff me. Don't do it, Fando. *(She sobs.)*

FANDO *(ruthlessly)*. Don't cry.

LIS *(making an effort not to cry)*. No, I won't cry, but don't handcuff me.

FANDO *(irritated)*. You're always suspicious of me.

LIS *(gently)*. No, I'm not suspicious of you. *(Full of sincerity, she adds.)* I believe you.

Fando walks a few steps from the pram to Lis. She is crying.

FANDO *(authoritatively)*. Give me your hands.

LIS. No, don't do it, Fando, don't handcuff me.

Lis holds out her hands. Fando handcuffs her nervously.

FANDO. It's better like that.

LIS. Fando. *(Very sadly.)* Fando.

FANDO. I put them on you to see if you can crawl with them on. Come on, try and crawl.

LIS. I can't Fando.

FANDO. Try.

LIS. Fando, don't hurt me.

FANDO *(beside himself)*. I tell you to try. Crawl.

Lis tries to crawl but she can't; her handcuffed hands prevent her.

LIS. I can't, Fando.

FANDO. Try, or worse things will happen to you.

LIS *(gently)*. Don't beat me, Fando, don't beat me.

FANDO. Try, I tell you.

Lis makes a great effort without success.

LIS. I can't, Fando.

FANDO. Try again.

LIS. I can't, Fando. Leave me alone. Don't hurt me.

FANDO. Try, or even worse things will happen to you.

LIS. Don't beat me. Whatever you do, don't beat me with the strap.

FANDO *(irritated)*. Try.

LIS. I can't.

Fando goes over to the pram and gets a strap out of it.

FANDO. Try, or I'll beat you.

LIS. Fando, don't beat me. I'm ill.

Fando beats Lis violently.

FANDO. Crawl.

Lis makes a supreme effort and manages to crawl. Fando watches her, quivering with excitement.

LIS. I can't any more.

FANDO. Go on, go on.

LIS. Don't beat me any more.

FANDO. Crawl.

Fando hits her again. Lis crawls, swaying from side to side. She makes an awkward movement and her chained hands bang into the drum and tear the parchment.

(furious). You've torn my drum. You've torn my drum.

Fando hits her. She falls down in a faint, she spits blood. Fando, irritated, takes the drum, moves away from her and starts to mend it with a needle and thread. Lis is stretched out, motionless, her chained hands on her breast, in the middle of the stage. Long silence. Fando works. Enter the three men with the umbrella. They go up to the woman. They study her very attentively and walk round her. Fando, absorbed in mending his drum, doesn't see them, and they don't notice him either.

MITARO. Look what she's got on her hands.

NAMUR *(lifting up Lis's hands to get a good look at the handcuffs).* They're handcuffs.

MITARO. They do look nice.

NAMUR. Not so very.

MITARO. Why do you have to contradict me?

TOSO *(interrupting them in a neutral voice).* She's got blood on her mouth.

Mitaro and Namur look carefully at Lis's mouth.

MITARO. It's quite true.

NAMUR. Now that's odd.

Namur gets hold of Lis's lips with his fingers as if with pincers and opens her mouth. Mitaro puts his finger in her mouth. Then he takes it out and smells it.

MITARO. It's the smell of blood.

NAMUR. How strange it all is.

Mitaro touches Lis's teeth.

MITARO. Look what little teeth she has! aren't they hard!

NAMUR. Teeth always are hard.

Mitaro gets hold of Lis's tongue and pulls it out.

MITARO. Look how pretty her tongue is! Isn't it velvety!

NAMUR. Tongues always are like that.

MITARO. You always have to say *something*.

Mitaro and Namur stop touching Lis's mouth. They now lift up her skirts and look carefully at her knees.

MITARO. What knees!

NAMUR. Like any other knees.

Mitaro runs over the topography of Lis's knees with his fingers.

MITARO. Look at the dimple here.

Namur explores the dimple while Toso sticks his ear to Lis's chest and listens carefully.

TOSO *(coldly)*. She's dead.

MITARO. There you go again with your silly tales.

TOSO *(coldly)*. She's dead because you can't hear her heart beating any more.

MITARO. Go on!

TOSO. And she isn't breathing any more.

Namur presses his ear to Lis's chest.

NAMUR. Well it's true, you can't hear her heart beating any more.

MITARO. She's dead, then?

TOSO. Of course.

NAMUR. We'll have to tell Fando.

MITARO. Naturally.

Namur and Mitaro go over to Fando who's working ener-getically trying to sew up the torn drum.

NAMUR *(to Fando)*. You know, Lis is dead.

FANDO *(dumbfounded)*. Lis is dead?

NAMUR. Yes.

Fando goes over towards Lis. He looks at her in awe and very sadly draws nearer to her. He embraces her, and sits her up. Lis's head falls back inertly. Fando says nothing. (The three men with the umbrella are standing solemnly and have taken their hats off.) Fando lays her back on the ground very carefully. Fando is on the verge of tears. Suddenly he presses his forehead to Lis's stomach. Although nothing can be heard, it is very likely that he is crying.

Curtain

Scene Five

The three men with the umbrella are on the stage.

MITARO. He'd promised her that when she died he'd go and see her in the cemetery with a flower and a dog.

NAMUR. No, that wasn't it. What happened was that she'd told him that she wanted to commit suicide and he'd answered that that was the best thing she could do. So she and the two men had killed the ticket man so that they could pay for the hire of the box-tricycle. And then they went to buy themselves some anchovy sandwiches and pay for hiring it but the police came and though they couldn't see any harm in it they took them away.

MITARO. Yes, I remember that one of them spent all his time sleeping and that he said he didn't want to think because it was a bore and that then his friend told him he'd do better to think of some funny stories and that he replied that he didn't know any . . . (*Thinking.*) But that's quite a different story. The one I'm talking about is the story of the man who was pushing a paralysed woman in a pram and trying to get to Tar. I remember that he said that he had been told that it was very difficult to get to Tar but that they would try, but later on he said that when they arrived he would compose lots of nice songs for her like the feather song and that he'd play them to her with the drum and it was then that they kissed each other.

NAMUR. No, it was then that she discovered that he was carrying a pair of handcuffs in his pocket and that he was going to put them on her. He said that they were nothing, but he kept them. Then she got cross and told him that. . . .

MITARO. No, you're altering everything, you're forgetting everything and you're mixing everything up. What happened was that afterwards a policeman arrived and we couldn't understand him very well and that the old flute-player said that he didn't understand him because he was so terribly stupid and the other chap got furious. (*Pause.*) And afterwards, that was when the two men arrived, one of whom played the harmonium and the other the typewriter.

NAMUR. Oh, yes, I remember them well, they were in a market-place somewhere. And their life was very sad because they couldn't swop instruments.

MITARO. Oh, yes they could, though, yes they could.

NAMUR. But that was after. And then suddenly the intelligent man came along and he showed them everything he knew and they couldn't get over it.

MITARO. No, no, what happened then was that she and he started playing at thinking. But as he didn't know how to get in the right position he thought very badly, and when she showed him what position he ought to put himself in he couldn't think of anything but death.

TOSO. What happened was that we got under an umbrella and tried to go to Tar. But you argued so much about what precautions we ought to take that when we finally left we were very late, as always.

Namur and Mitaro have been showing obvious boredom as they listened to Toso.

NAMUR *(interrupting him)*. And what's all that got to do with anything?

MITARO. You see how you always disturb us.

Toso is silent.

NAMUR. There's nothing to be done with him.

MITARO. We mustn't take any more notice of him—no more than if he didn't exist.

NAMUR. Where'd we got to?

MITARO. I was saying that he'd promised to go and see her in the cemetery with a flower and a dog.

NAMUR. No, that was earlier. What I was telling you was that it made the girl sad when she saw that he couldn't play the ass, even with his tail.

MITARO. Yes, that was it, it made her sad. *(He ponders.)* But what happened was that he pulled up her skirts to attract the ticket man and then the man went over to them and they sprang a trap and killed him.

NAMUR. No, my dear chap, no; what happened was that they couldn't find any way of classifying it all and, what's more, they were worried because she'd told them that if she thought it was a bad plan she'd say so without any regard for anybody's feelings. And it was then that he decided that the best thing to do would be to measure everything.

Enter Fando with a flower and a dog on a raffia lead. The men with the umbrella stop speaking and follow him with their eyes as he slowly crosses the stage without speaking and without stopping.—Perhaps he's tired: he looks it.

We'll go with him.

MITARO. Yes.

TOSO. And when shall we go to Tar?

NAMUR. We must go with him first. Then we'll all four start.

MITARO. Yes, all together.

The three men under the umbrella start walking behind Fando. In the middle of the stage they stop and take their hats off. Then they immediately start walking again and go off.

Curtain

THE CAR CEMETERY

CHARACTERS

LASCA, *An elderly woman*

TIOSSODO, *A very young man*

MILOS, *A manservant, about 40*

DILA, *A young woman of 25*

EMANOU, *A trumpeter, 33*

TOPÉ, *Clarinetist, about 30*

FODÈRE, *Saxophonist, about 30*

A play in two acts

ACT ONE

The action takes place in a large space in front of a car cemetery. At the back, cars. Many cars piled on top of the other can be seen perfectly in the distance because of the different levels of the ground. The cars are all old, dirty and rusted.

All those in the first row have curtains made of sackcloth instead of windows. To differentiate them they are called: Car 1, Car 2, Car 3, Car 4 and Car 5. In front, and on the stage R, is Car A. It also has sackcloth curtains instead of windows. On the roof of this car there is a chimney. In front of Car 2, a pair of very dirty, worn-out boots.

An athlete enters from the right at the double. It is Tiossodo, who is a caricature of an athlete; his bearing is also a caricature of athleticism. He is dressed as an athlete; he is very young. He wears the number 456 on his chest. He will cross the stage from right to left.

Lasca sometimes follows him and sometimes slightly precedes him. Lasca is an elderly woman, she is dressed fairly ordinarily; she has white hair. She seems to be indefatigable. She gives all sorts of advice to Tiossodo.

LASCA. Your chest. *(After a short pause.)* Your breathing, don't forget, take a breath. Your chin. *(After a short pause.)* Don't forget your breathing.

Lasca is indefatigable. Tiossodo appears more and more exhausted. They cross the stage from right to left, and go out left. Silence. Suddenly some noises can be heard coming from Car 3. A candle is lit inside it. A faint glow can be seen through the sackcloth curtain. In Car 3 a man and a woman of about 70, invisible to the audience, are talking.

WOMAN'S VOICE. What's the matter, my angel?

MAN'S VOICE. I can't sleep. Something's getting in my way.

WOMAN'S VOICE. It must be the steering wheel sticking into your back again.

MAN'S VOICE. No, that's not it. I'm in the wrong place.

WOMAN'S VOICE. Would you like to change places with me?

MAN'S VOICE. If you like.

A great hullabaloo. Noises of rusty springs, of old iron, of pushing and shoving. The man's and the woman's voices: "Come on, now," "Don't push," "It's not me that's pushing," "Mind my leg," "ow," etc. After a few groans denoting effort, peace is re-established.

WOMAN'S VOICE. Are you all right, my angel?

MAN'S VOICE. Yes, much better.

WOMAN'S VOICE. Do you want anything else?

MAN'S VOICE. No, perhaps we'll be able to sleep in peace now. *(Very short pause.)* Did you ask them to bring us our breakfast tomorrow morning?

WOMAN'S VOICE. Oh, no, I forgot. Never mind, I'll call the man now.

The horn of Car 3 is heard. Then it sounds again. From Car A comes a very well-dressed manservant. His name is Milos. He goes over to Car 3. He sticks his head under the sackcloth curtain.

MILOS. What can I do for you, madam?

WOMAN'S VOICE. We forgot to order our breakfast.

MILOS. Do you and the gentleman wish for breakfast in bed, madam?

WOMAN'S VOICE. Of course.

MILOS. And what will you be taking for breakfast, madam?

WOMAN'S VOICE *(to her husband)*. What would you like?

MAN'S VOICE. A glass of red wine.

WOMAN'S VOICE. Bring us two glasses of red wine, then.

MILOS. I'm extremely sorry, madam, sir, but we haven't any red wine.

MAN'S VOICE *(sounding irritated)*. No red wine! What kind of a dump have we got ourselves into? No red wine! I told you I didn't like this place. But you would insist. *(To Milos.)* What *have* you got, then?

MILOS. We have chewing gum, chicory, one wafer, some bread and some liquorice.

MAN'S VOICE. And water—have you any water?

MILOS. Yes, sir, as much as you wish.

MAN'S VOICE. Well then, bring us three glasses of really warm water each.

MILOS. Would you like small glasses, sir, or large ones?

MAN'S VOICE. Large ones.

MILOS. And would you and madam like anything else, sir?

MAN'S VOICE. No, that's all.

MILOS. If there is anything else you and madam would like, sir, I am at your disposition. Just call me. I wish you a good night, sir, madam.

Milos goes back to Car A. He notices the pair of boots at the door of Car 2. He picks them up, examines them and puts them back. He takes a brush out of Car A. He goes back to Car 2. He picks up one of the boots. He spits on it, very elegantly, then he applies himself to spreading the saliva all over the boot with the brush. Finally he makes the boots shine.
While he's polishing them, Lasca and Tiossodo enter from right. Tiossodo is still dressed as an athlete, he still moves at the double, and he seems even more exhausted than before. Lasca, fresher than ever, goes on lavishing advice on Tiossodo.

LASCA. Your breathing! Take a breath! *(Pause.)* Stick your chest out! *(Pause.)* Stand up straight, don't hunch your back. *(Pause.)* Your breathing! Take a breath!

They cross the stage from right to left. They go out left. Milos hasn't even noticed they were there. He continues indefatigably to clean the boots, without for a moment losing his air of breeding. When he has finished cleaning the boots, he goes back to Car A. Before he gets into the car Dila, a young woman, appears from the right. She goes towards Car A. Milos stands in her way.

MILOS. Go and do what I told you to.

DILA. Let me off just for today.

MILOS *(angry)*. Hold out your hand.

Dila submits, timidly. Milos hits her on the fingers with a cane.

And again!

Dila holds her hand out to Milos once again. He again hits her fingers.

And again! *(As before.)* And now go and do what I told you to.

Dila, almost in tears, goes over to Car 1. She sticks her head under the sackcloth curtain. Milos, who is standing near Car A watches her.

DILA. Excuse me, sir, may I kiss you on the mouth. *(Noise of a kiss.)* Thank you.

Dila, still on the verge of tears, goes over to Car 2. She puts her head under the curtain.

Aren't you asleep yet? Why not?

MAN'S VOICE. Why don't you bloody well leave me in peace. I've had enough of this nonsense you go in for every evening.

DILA. Kiss me.

MAN'S VOICE. I've already said no a thousand times, do I have to say it again?

DILA. Then let me kiss you.

MAN'S VOICE. Leave me alone, I tell you.

It seems as if Dila is forcing herself to kiss him all the same. She doesn't seem to be able to manage it. Milos watches with an air of satisfaction. Dila goes over to Car 3. She puts her head under the curtain. She is heard kissing someone. The following dialogue then starts.

WOMAN'S VOICE. What is it?

MAN'S VOICE. Nothing.

Dila goes over to Car 4. She puts her head under the curtain. A kiss is heard.

MAN'S VOICE. One more. *(A kiss is heard.)* And another. *(A kiss is heard.)* Thank you.

Dila goes over to Car 5. Milos is still watching her with a satisfied air.

DILA. Excuse me, sir, please kiss me on the mouth. *(Kiss.)* Thank you.

Dila, nearly in tears, goes back to Milos.

MILOS. And don't let me catch you forgetting my orders again.

Dila, on the verge of tears, doesn't answer. They both go over to Car A. Milos puts his arm round Dila's shoulders very affectionately. They go into Car A. Silence.
Tiossodo enters, right, at the double, even more exhausted than before. Lasca sometimes precedes him and sometimes follows very closely behind him, marking time.

LASCA. One, two, 1, 2, 1, 2, 1, 2, 1, 2, 1, 2, 1, 2, 1, 2. . . .

They cross the stage from right to left. They disappear left. Silence.
Emanou enters, left, a trumpet in his hand. In his other hand he carries a work-basket. He plays an Armstrong blues on his trumpet. His trumpet reverberates for a long time in the silence.
When Emanou starts playing, Dila, looking pleased, puts her head out of the door and looks at him very enthusiastically. Milos violently closes the sackcloth curtain again and pulls Dila back into Car A.

A pause. Silence.
At the back, right, a clarinet is heard playing. Emanou starts playing again.
Silence.
At the back, left, someone starts playing a saxophone. Immediately afterwards, the clarinet is heard, then Emanou's trumpet.
Silence.
Topé enters, right, a clarinet in his hand. Fodère enters, left, with a saxophone in one hand and three folded-up hammocks in the other.
Fodère is dumb. They greet each other merrily.

EMANOU. I've been waiting for you for quite a time.

TOPÉ. You can't say we're late.

Fodère unrolls the three hammocks. The three friends sit down on them and make themselves comfortable. Though Fodère is dumb he can express himself very well. His dumb show is very gay. He is almost always on the side of Emanou, whom he greatly admires. Emanou takes out of his work-basket everything that is needed for knitting; he is making a pullover. Fodère winds the wool that Topé is holding on his wrists.

TOPÉ. Do you know what time we have to play?

EMANOU. Yes, soon.

TOPÉ. It's tonight the cops are supposed to arrest us, isn't it?

EMANOU. So I've heard. *(Pause.)* We'll run away.

TOPÉ. Will the dance go on for long?

EMANOU. Till dawn.

Topé. We're going to have to play a hell of a lot !

Emanou. But we've got to do it.

Topé. We ought to try another profession—a better paid one.

Emanou. I've already thought of that.

Topé. And ?

Emanou. We could be burglars.

Topé. Burglars ?

Emanou. Yes.

Topé *(surprised and pleased)*. No ?

Emanou. If we were, we'd have lots of money.

Topé. Good Lord, so we would.

Emanou. And we'd be important people.

Topé *(suddenly)*. And could we be murderers too ?

Emanou. Why not ?

Topé *(looking pleased)*. They'd talk about us in the papers.

Emanou. Of course they would.

Topé. But it wouldn't be easy for us to be burglars.

Emanou. No, but we can try.

Topé. And even less to be murderers.

Emanou. Yes, that's even more difficult. And then you have to have some luck.

TOPÉ. It's obvious that murdering someone can't be as simple as people like to think.

EMANOU. Far from it. There's always a great hullabaloo; bloodstains, fingerprints. . . .

TOPÉ *(interrupting him with a foolish laugh)*. Ah yes, fingerprints, I've heard of them before.

EMANOU. It's very complicated. And then the victim almost always starts screaming, from what I've heard.

TOPÉ. Screaming?

EMANOU. Yes, he doesn't want you to kill him.

TOPÉ. That must be wonderful.

EMANOU. Yes, but I told you : it's very difficult and very dangerous.

TOPÉ. And can't anyone kill anyone without getting caught?

EMANOU. Of course they can. It's all very well organised, but you have to study a lot of different things.

TOPÉ. How come?

EMANOU. We could be judges.

TOPÉ. And we'd earn just as much money as we would if we were murderers.

EMANOU. Yes.

TOPÉ. And who do judges kill, then?

EMANOU. Oh, that's very simple—they kill people who do things that aren't right.

TOPÉ. And how do they manage to know that they're not right?

EMANOU. They're very intelligent.

TOPÉ *(amazed)*. They must be. *(Pause.)* But do they always, always, always know that they're bad?

EMANOU. Yes, always, always, always. I told you, they're very intelligent, and then they study a lot of subjects, at the very least they've passed their baccalaureat and all that.

TOPÉ *(amazed)*. Ah yes, in that case, yes.

Someone sounds the horn in Car 2. Emanou and Topé stop talking and wait. The horn sounds twice more.
Milos comes out of Car A, still impeccably dressed as a man-servant. The three friends watch. Milos goes over to Car 2. He puts his head under the sackcloth curtain.

MILOS. Is there something you want, sir?

MAN'S VOICE *(curt and authoritative)*. Yes, a woman.

MILOS. I'll bring one right away, sir. Is there anything else you want, sir? *(Silence.)* Then I wish you a good night, sir.

Milos goes into Car A. Dila, on the verge of tears, immediately comes out and goes over to Car 2. She puts her head under the curtain.

DILA. Good evening, sir.

Before she can finish her sentence, a hand pulls her inside with some violence. Dila disappears into Car 2. Emanou, Topé and Fodère have been watching with curiosity, but without the slightest surprise.

TOPÉ. You know, Emanou, this business of playing every night, neverendingly, is beginning to get me down.

EMANOU. But the poor must dance too, Topé. And as they haven't any money to go to a dance-hall. . . .

TOPÉ. Yes, of course, and at our expense.

EMANOU. No, my dear chap, we can play, so how can it hurt us to play so that the poor people in the neighbourhood can dance?

TOPÉ. Yes, once, twicé, even for a year if you like. But how many years is it that we've had to come every night?

EMANOU. It's a long time since I stopped counting them.

TOPÉ. Me too. And anyway, as it isn't allowed, then we're running the risk of being put in prison when we least expect it. It's quite certain that they'll come and arrest us tonight, you know.

EMANOU. Don't worry. Our pals will tip us off and we'll be able to beat it.

TOPÉ. It's too risky. And anyway, as if that wasn't enough, we have to knit them pullovers for the winter as well, and buy them daisies so's they can tell if their girl friends love them or not when they're in love.

EMANOU. Don't forget that we have to be good.

TOPÉ. You're always telling me that. But what do we get out of it?

EMANOU. Well, when we're good *(he recites this as if he's learnt a lesson by heart)* we experience a great inner joy born of peace of spirit that is revealed to us when we see that we resemble the ideal man.

Topé *(enthusiastically)*. You're a marvellous chap! You never go the slightest bit wrong! And what's more, you say it all in one breath, and that's even more difficult.

Emanou. Of course : I learnt it by heart.

Silence.

Topé. Personally I think that if you wanted to see that the poor don't suffer you'd have to kill them all.

Emanou. That's not possible. The others have been trying for a long time and they can't manage it, and yet they're powerful people.

Topé. Then there isn't any solution.

Emanou. No, there isn't any. We'll have to go on playing every night.

Topé. The trouble is that the others resent it, as you well know. Ever since you fed all the dancers with just one loaf and a tin of sardines the other day, they can't stand you any more. Neither they nor the cops will allow you a moment's peace.

Tiossodo enters right, at the double, exhausted by his exertions. Lasca follows him, indefatigable, and gives him advice. She carries a large alarm clock.

Lasca. Just one more little effort and you'll beat the record. *(Pause.)* Just one more tiny little effort and you'll beat the record. *(Pause.)* Go on, go on. *(Pause.)* You'll see—this time you really will beat the record.

Lasca and Tiossodo cross the stage from right to left. They go out left. While Lasca and Tiossodo have been crossing the stage the three friends have stopped talking and have been watching them curiously, but without the slightest surprise.

EMANOU. But if we don't play, who *will* play?

TOPÉ. Well yes, you're right there.

EMANOU. And then, what with it being so cold at night at the moment, if they don't dance, you can imagine. . . .

TOPÉ. You don't need to tell *me* that, I'm like an icicle when I play the clarinet.

EMANOU. And I've told you a thousand times that it's not permanent work. As soon as we find something more profitable for them and less tiring for us we'll make a change.

From the wings, left, can be heard irritated voices saying: "Well what about those musicians, are they going to come or aren't they?" "Are they going to arrive a bit later every evening?" "They're really going too far." (In Chorus.) *"Mu-sic! Mu-sic! Mu-sic! Mu-sic!"*

TOPÉ. You hear them?

EMANOU. You're quite right, they're fed up.

TOPÉ. And if we don't start right away I don't know what they're not capable of doing.

EMANOU. Just let me finish my row. *(He knits rapidly so as to finish his row as quickly as possible.)*

Voices can still be heard, becoming more and more violent.

ALL TOGETHER. But what can those blasted musicians be doing, why aren't they here?

TOPÉ. Look, come on, they're going to lynch us.

EMANOU. Yes, they're pretty violent. And you should just see them when they get really worked up!

TOPÉ. Of course; it's our fault, we ought to be down there.

EMANOU. You go. I'll join you when I've finished my row.

TOPÉ. Right. See you in a minute.

Topé and Fodère go out, right. Soon the men who were shouting start whistling. There is some isolated clapping all the same. Shortly afterwards the music starts. The tunes are played fairly softly. Only jazz and rock 'n' roll.
As soon as Topé and Fodère have gone off, Emanou runs to the right to make sure that his friends have really gone and then immediately goes over to Car 2.

EMANOU *(in a murmur)*. Dila! Dila!

Silence.

(as before). Dila! Dila! It's me.

MAN'S VOICE *(from inside Car 2, contemptuously)*. Wait a bit, hell. She's coming out in a minute.

Silence. Emanou waits very impatiently. Finally Dila puts her head out. She is getting ready to come out. Suddenly a hand pulls her back inside. Silence. Emanou waits impatiently. Finally Dila comes out of Car 2, this time with some violence, probably pushed from inside. She falls down. Emanou goes over to her.

EMANOU. I wanted to see you. *(Pause.)* Dila, I want to sleep with you.

DILA *(surprised)*. Now?

EMANOU. Yes. My friends say I'm not a man. They say I can't be one so long as I haven't been with a woman.

DILA. And you want it to be me?

EMANOU. Yes, Dila, you're better than the others. With you I shall only feel just a little ashamed. And I know more or less what to do.

DILA. But you know how jealous he is.

EMANOU. He won't see us. And if he does see us we'll tell him we're playing soldiers.

DILA. But Emanou, you've got to go and play the trumpet for the dancing.

EMANOU. No, not tonight. And anyway it won't take a minute. Don't you want to?

DILA. Yes, but. . . .

EMANOU. Oh I see, you don't want to because you know I haven't had any experience.

DILA. That doesn't matter, I've had a lot.

EMANOU. Well then, Dila, we offset each other.

DILA. Come on then.

Dila and Emanou go behind Car A so that the audience can't see them. At the dance, back right, they are at this moment playing rock 'n' roll. Soon Milos comes out of Car A. He climbs on to the engine of Car A and watches what's going on behind it, that is to say what Dila and Emanou are doing. He watches them with curiosity and satisfaction. Shortly afterwards he goes over to Car 2. He speaks to the man inside it, putting his head under the sackcloth curtain.

MILOS. Look what Dila's doing. *(He laughs.)* Mind she doesn't see you. Look through the curtains *(He laughs.)*

Milos partially hides behind Car 2. The boisterous laugh of the man in Car 2 is heard. Milos now puts his head under the sackcloth curtain of Car 3.

Look. Just look. *(He laughs.)* If you hide behind the curtains you can see everything very well.

Milos partially hides behind Car 3. The man in Car 2 is heard laughing. The couple in Car 3 are also heard laughing.

WOMAN'S VOICE *(Car 3, her words interspersed with laughter)*. Isn't it amusing?

MAN'S VOICE *(Car 3, words interspersed with laughter)*. Isn't it funny! It's a really funny sight!

Laughter from everybody. Milos goes over to Car 1, and puts his head under the sackcloth curtain. He must be whispering something very amusing to the man inside it. The people in Cars 1, 2 and 3 laugh more and more.
Tiossodo enters, right, at the double. This time, though he is just as exhausted as he was before, he is marking time with his head. Lasca indefatigable, lavishes her advice on him. She is now by Tiossodo's side. Their heads are almost touching. Lasca marks time like Tiossodo.

LASCA. One, two, 1, 2, 1, 2, 1, 2, 1, 2, 1, 2. We're getting on, we're getting on towards the record. One, two, 1, 2, 1, 2. We're getting on.

Lasca and Tiossodo, having crossed the stage from right to left, go out, left. While they have been crossing the stage the laughter has stopped. It starts again without the slightest inhibition.
Milos goes up to Cars 4 and 5 one after the other. He says to the people inside.

Milos. Look, just look. *(He laughs.)* Look how funny it is.

None of the people in Cars 1, 2, 3, 4 and 5 can be seen. But their laughter can be heard for some time. All of a sudden, the laughter stops. Milos goes back to Car A looking frightened. Climbing on to the engine he looks once more at what is going on behind the car. Once again he looks as if he is terror-stricken. Finally he goes into Car A. Long silence. Dila and Emanou reappear. They come out from behind Car A.

Emanou *(guiltily)*. Dila . . . the truth is that my pals have never said anything to me . . . and anyway, I *have* had some experience. But I wanted to go with you.

Dila. Why do you tell me the same old story every evening?

Emanou. Don't be cross with me, Dila.

Dila. You don't need to invent anything, you've known for a long time that I always say yes.

Emanou. Yes, but I have to be careful. I promise I'll never deceive you again.

Dila. You make the same promise every evening.

Emanou. This time I swear I'll mend my ways.

Dila. I still trust you. But. . . .

Emanou. I want to be good, Dila.

Dila. I want to be good, too, Emanou.

Emanou. You already are: you let everybody sleep with you.

Dila. I'd like to be even better.

EMANOU. So would I.

DILA. But where will it get us—being good?

EMANOU. Well, when we're good *(he recites this as if he's learnt a lesson by heart)* we experience a great inner joy born of the peace of spirit that is revealed to us when we see that we resemble the ideal man.

DILA *(enthusiastically)*. You say it better every time.

EMANOU *(proudly)*. Yes, I needn't grumble. I've learnt it by heart.

DILA. You're terribly intelligent—you know everything.

EMANOU *(modestly)*. Not everything, but nearly everything. The important things, at any rate, and always by heart.

DILA. I think there's something in you that's different from everybody else. *(Pause.)* Just tell me some of the things you know.

EMANOU. Well I know . . . what the point of being good is . . . I know how to play the trumpet. I know the months of the year without leaving any of them out. . . .

DILA. No?

EMANOU. Yes . . . and then I know how much all the different bank notes are worth . . . I know the days of the week by heart too. . . .

DILA. You're a marvellous chap! And, do you know how to think things and prove things like important people do?

EMANOU. Yes, I have a special method for that. Tell me the most difficult thing you can think of to prove to you.

DILA. Prove to me that giraffes go up in lifts.

EMANOU. Giraffes go up in lifts because they go up in lifts.

DILA *(enthusiastically)*. How well you proved it !

EMANOU. I prove everything just as well.

DILA. You really are clever. *(Pause.)* And what if I were to ask you to prove the opposite; that giraffes don't go up in lifts?

EMANOU. That would be even easier : I should only have to prove it in the same way, only the other way round.

DILA. Oh! Very good! You can do everything. I tell you, you must have something in you, or else you must be the son *(she points to the sky and says awkwardly)* . . . of someone, of someone, what shall I say, who's in a very high position.

EMANOU. No. My mother was poor. She told me that she was so poor that when I was just about to be born no one wanted to take her in. It was only a little cow and a baby donkey who were in a very poor sort of cow-shed who took pity on her. So my mother went into the cow-shed and I was born. The ass and the cow kept me warm with their breath. The cow was pleased to see me born and she went "Moo! Moo!", and the donkey brayed and waggled his ears.

DILA. Didn't anyone want to listen to your mother?

EMANOU. No. Afterwards she left for another village and my father was a carpenter there. I helped him make tables and chairs and wardrobes. But in the evenings I learnt to play the trumpet. And when I was thirty I told my father and mother that I was going to play the trumpet so that people who didn't have any money could still go out dancing in the evenings.

DILA. Was it then that your friends joined you?

EMANOU. Yes.

The music, which has been playing up to now, stops: the jazz piece is finished. Shouts are heard, coming from the back right. It is Topé calling.

TOPÉ. Emanou ! Emanou ! Emanou ! Emanou !

EMANOU. I must go or they'll get cross.

Fodère enters from the right, running. He makes a sign to Emanou to come, that they are waiting for him.

Good-bye Dila, I'll see you soon.

DILA. Good-bye, Emanou. *(Suddenly anxious.)* Hey, are the cops going to be looking for you tonight ?

EMANOU. I think so. Will you tip us off ?

DILA. Of course.

EMANOU. Thank you. Good-bye.

DILA. Good-bye.

Emanou and Fodère go off together right. Soon the music can be heard again; jazz, rock 'n' roll. Dila is alone on the stage. She knocks loudly on the door of Car A.

Come out of there, it's no good hiding. Will you come out, you idiot.

After a short while Milos comes out, hanging his head and looking apprehensive.

Don't hang your head. Look at me. *(With growing violence.)* I tell you to look at me. Can't you hear? Hold your head up.

Milos fearfully raises his head.

How many times have I told you to leave me in peace?

MILOS. Dila, I didn't know that. . . .

DILA. Huh, so you didn't know, eh? Every evening I have to tell you the same thing. You think this little game can go on a long time. I've had enough. I'm going for good.

MILOS (*imploring her*). No, Dila, don't leave me alone, don't go.

DILA. And as if that wasn't enough, you had to tell all those half-wits! (*She points to the cars. Silence. To the people in the cars.*) That's right, butter wouldn't melt in your mouth, would it? What do you think? . . . that I don't know that you spy on me from behind your curtains?

In Car 3 an apprehensive whispering can be heard. The curtains of cars move imperceptibly.

What's that you're saying? Have the guts to say something. Why are you laughing?

Silence. Dila goes over to Car 2. She lifts up the curtain. There is no one inside.

So you suddenly fell asleep, eh? D'you think I didn't hear you roaring with laughter just now?

MILOS. Leave them alone, you know they're heavy sleepers. It's no use your talking to them, they won't hear you.

DILA. They won't hear me! There's none so deaf as those who don't want to hear.

Silence. Whispers are heard coming from inside the cars. The sackcloth curtains move.

What's that you're saying? Just have the guts to say it to me.

Silence.

MILOS. Leave them alone, Dila, you know how nervous and sensitive they are. It'd be better for them not to wake up.

DILA. That's right, stand up for *them* now, as if you didn't have enough to do to stand up for yourself.

MILOS. No, Dila, no, I'm not standing up for them. *(Pause.)* Let me go to bed. I'm very sleepy.

DILA. So his lordship is very sleepy, eh? His lordship can't stay out a minute longer.

MILOS. No, Dila, I can't any more, I'm very sleepy. You know that there's an enormous amount of work to do in the mornings. I have to serve them their breakfasts in bed, I have to clean out the cars, make the beds, do the housework, polish the floors. You know how fussy they are. And if I don't go to sleep now I shan't even be capable of crawling tomorrow.

DILA. But ask me to forgive you first.

MILOS. Yes, Dila, forgive me.

DILA. On your knees, and say it better than that.

MILOS *(on his knees, sounding moved)*. Forgive me, Dila.

Giggles from inside the Cars.

DILA. You can go to bed.

Milos tries to kiss Dila good night. Dila pushes him away violently.

Don't touch me.

Milos goes over to Car A. He gets into the car. Silence. Dila goes over to Car 3.

(to people in Car 3). So you're still asleep, eh? *(Silence.)* Give me the mirror and comb; I want to do my hair. *(Silence.)* Didn't you hear what I said?

From the curtains of Car 3 a gigantic mirror and comb appear. The hand of the person holding them out cannot be seen. Dila grabs them, violently. Silence. Dila goes over to one of the hammocks. She sits down on it. She starts to do her hair with great care.

From the left—contrary to the previous occasions when they have come in from the right—Tiossodo and Lasca enter. Tiossodo is still dressed as an athlete; he crosses the stage from left to right. Lasca, indefatigable, appears to be dissatisfied with her pupil.

LASCA *(very dissatisfied: Tiossodo seems to be ignoring all her advice)*. But can't you hear me? I keep telling you, you're going in the wrong direction. If you do that, how d'you think you're going to beat the record? I tell you, turn left, you've made a mistake. Do you hear me?

Tiossodo suddenly stops. He hesitates for a minute. He looks as if he's trying to find his bearings. He's half asleep and very tired. Finally he changes course: he comes back towards the left, still at the double.

LASCA *(pleased)*. That's it. That's the right direction. You'll see, you'll beat the record. Your breathing! One, two, 1, 2, 1, 2, 1, 2, 1, 2, 1, 2....

Lasca and Tiossodo go out left. Dila continues calmly combing her hair. Milos puts his head through the sackcloth curtain of Car A. He looks at Dila and smiles. Dila raises her head. Milos timidly draws his head back as quickly as he can. A pause. Music can still be heard at the back. Suddenly, from far away on the left, voices are heard.

MAN'S VOICE. E-ma-nou! E-ma-nou! The cops! E-ma-nou! The cops!

ANOTHER MAN'S VOICE. E-ma-nou! The cops are here! They're coming!

Dila gets up and goes over towards left. She passes in front of Car A. Milos puts his head under the curtain.

MILOS. Don't go. Don't warn them. What does it matter to you if the cops get them? Don't get mixed up in it.

DILA (*violently*). I'm not a child. I can look after myself. (*She goes out left, calling.*) Emanou! The cops! . . .

Milos sorrowfully watches her go off. Finally he draws back his head. From the distance, left, come the sounds of police whistles. They are heard during the whole of the following scene.
From now on, and up to the end of the first act, the action in the wings will take place in precise counterpoint to the action that is seen on the stage.
Lasca and Tiossodo enter. Tiossodo is literally dragging himself along and is incapable of taking even one more step. Lasca, indefatigable, pushes and drags him to make him keep on. It must be remembered that Lasca is an elderly woman; she has white hair. Tiossodo is young.

LASCA. Make an effort. Just one. Just one more.

When they reach the middle of the stage, Tiossodo falls down, exhausted by all the effort. He has fainted. Lasca gives him artificial respiration. Then she carries him in her arms over to one of the hammocks. Tiossodo slowly regains consciousness.
While this has been happening the music has stopped. Cries of panic and the noise of people running are heard, right. Left, police whistles, coming nearer and nearer to the stage.

TIOSSODO (*coming to himself, tenderly to Lasca*). My darling!

LASCA. Don't get sentimental, the way you always do.

TIOSSODO. Kiss me, my darling. I need it.

LASCA (*without listening to him*). Do you feel all right? You don't feel faint any more?

TIOSSODO. No, my love. Now you are all I have.

Tiossodo tries to kiss Lasca passionately. She pushes him away violently.

LASCA. Not here. I've already told you a thousand times that you're not to behave like that in public.

TIOSSODO. Just one kiss. If you don't give me a kiss I won't be able to come to.

LASCA. Well only one, eh?

Tiossodo and Lasca kiss passionately and at length. While they are kissing, whispers and giggles can be heard in the cars and the curtains are seen to move. Back right, the sound of frantic running can still be heard. Back left, whistles still coming nearer. Tiossodo and Lasca stop kissing.

You don't think anyone saw us, do you?

TIOSSODO. No, Lasca, no one.

LASCA. I thought I heard some suspicious noises.

TIOSSODO. You have so much imagination, my love!

They again kiss passionately and lengthily. While they are kissing, Fodère, Topé and Emanou rapidly cross the stage from right to left all hunched up, their chins almost touching their knees. Topé stops and jumps up to try and see what's going on at the back behind the cars. He is horrified, and makes a sign to his friends to show them that the danger is behind the cars. And in fact the sound of whistles can be plainly heard behind the cars at the back. Topé, Fodère and Emanou, still hunched up, cross the stage and go out left. But the police whistles sound from further away towards the right. Lasca and Tiossodo stop kissing.

LASCA *(overflowing with love)*. Oh, Tiossodo, you're so wonderful!

TIOSSODO. Will you always love me?

LASCA. Yes, Tiossodo, you know I will.

TIOSSODO. Until I die?

LASCA. You can't die.

TIOSSODO. Nor can you, Lasca. We'll both live together.

LASCA. Do you love me as much as you did the first day?

TIOSSODO. Yes.

LASCA *(annoyed)*. Only as much as you did the first day?

TIOSSODO. No, much more.

Lasca kisses Tiossodo passionately. Whispers in the Cars. The sackcloth curtains move. In Car 3 a voice says "No, really though, are they going to start all over again?"
Sounds of whistles and running are still heard in the distance.

LASCA *(suddenly worried)*. Come on, you must go on with your training.

TIOSSODO *(very much annoyed)*. No, Lasca, that's enough for today.

LASCA. That's enough? You think that's enough? Have you by any chance forgotten that you only started at five in the morning today.

TIOSSODO. Just for once.

LASCA. Just for once? D'you think *that's* any excuse? You know perfectly well that you're supposed to start at four every morning. If you waste one hour that's the beginning of the end.

TIOSSODO. I'll make it up tomorrow. *(Pause. Tenderly.)* And anyway, today I hope to do something better.

LASCA *(horrified)*. Oh, no, not that. Certainly not. It takes too much out of you. If you go on like that you'll never be able to beat the record.

TIOSSODO *(beseeching her)*. Just once, Lasca.

LASCA. Out of the question.

TIOSSODO. But Lasca . . . when I'm with you. . . .

LASCA. No, I tell you, no. And anyway there's nowhere we could go.

TIOSSODO. We could go into a car.

LASCA. No, not that. Would you be capable of taking me in there? Is that the way you love me?

TIOSSODO. Only this once. No one will notice.

LASCA. But somebody might recognise me. And then if they go and tell my. . . .

TIOSSODO *(interrupting her)*. No one will see us. It's pitch dark.

LASCA. And you want me to fill up the registration form? When they send them God knows where! You never know *who* takes charge of them.

TIOSSODO. No, I'll fill up mine and that'll be that. You won't need to.

LASCA *(after a short silence, on the verge of tears)*. And anyway, I know very well that afterwards you'll behave like a brute.

TIOSSODO. No, Lasca, I'll be very gentle.

LASCA. But will you still love me afterwards, or will you be like all men are?

TIOSSODO. No, Lasca, I'm not like the others. You'll see. Let's go.

Tiossodo and Lasca go over to Car A. Lasca timidly hides behind the engine. Tiossodo knocks on the door of Car A. Silence. Tiossodo knocks again.

MILOS' VOICE *(he has apparently just woken up)*. All right, all right, I'm coming. You don't need to knock so loudly, I'm not deaf.

No one comes. A pause. Shortly afterwards, back right Dila is heard saying: "Emanou, the cops are coming back". Police whistles are then heard, getting nearer. Left, frantic running. Dila goes on calling to Emanou to warn him that the police are coming.
Tiossodo and Lasca grow impatient.

LASCA. Well are they going to open the door, or aren't they?

TIOSSODO. Don't get impatient, for goodness' sake.

LASCA. Knock again.

Tiossodo knocks, trying not to make any noise.

MILOS' VOICE *(he has apparently just woken up)*. I tell you, I'm coming. What a lot! What a way to knock!

No one comes. From the right whistles can still be heard, coming nearer. Left, the sound of running. Finally, from left, Fodère, Topé and Emanou enter. All three are hurrying but walk hunched up so that they can't be seen. They cross the stage from left to right and go out right. The sounds of the whistles now move towards the back, behind the cars. Tiossodo and Lasca get more and more impatient.

LASCA. Knock again.

Tiossodo knocks very gently on the door of Car A.

MILOS' VOICE *(he has apparently just woken up)*. All right, I'm coming. Did you think I didn't hear you? If you go on thumping like a deaf man you'll break my car to bits.

A pause. The whistles get further away, back left; the noise of running moves over to the right. The noise decreases. Finally Milos' head appears.

MILOS *(brusquely)*. What d'you want?

TIOSSODO. I'd like to stay the night here.

MILOS *(suddenly obsequious)*. Oh, please excuse me for keeping you waiting, sir, I didn't think it was a client. We have the very thing for you at the moment, sir.

TIOSSODO. But . . . I'm not alone.

MILOS. You have someone with you. That doesn't matter. There's room. Have you an identity card?

TIOSSODO. Well, no, I forgot it, it's at home.

MILOS *(brutal and suspicious again)*. Then there's nothing for you, bloody hell.

TIOSSODO. Would my athlete's number be any use? *(He tears off the number 456 which he wears on his chest and gives it to Milos.)*

MILOS *(very polite and obliging once more)*. Well, naturally. We're here to serve you, sir, and to oblige you. Sign here please.

Tiossodo signs. Once again Dila's voice is heard "Emanou, the cops are coming back." This time the noises of whistles and running come from the right. They are getting nearer.

Milos. If you will kindly follow me, sir, madam.

Lasca. But isn't he going to ask me to fill up a form?

Milos. The gentleman's will be enough.

Lasca. But I must fill one in too.

Milos. Please don't worry, madam, the gentleman's form will be sufficient.

Lasca *(angry)*. Very well. You know your job better than I do. Personally I don't care. But you'll be sorry.

Milos ceremoniously opens the door of Car 2 for them.

Milos *(to man in Car 2)*. This lady and gentleman are going to occupy the other half, sir.

Man's voice. The bastards! Can't they go and fornicate elsewhere?

Milos. I'm extremely sorry, sir; I'll try and find you a car to yourself tomorrow.

Man's voice. You certainly know how to mess people around.

Tiossodo and Lasca go into Car 2. Before the door is shut, Lasca says to Milos.

Lasca. Call us at three tomorrow morning.

Milos. As you wish, madam. I wish you a good night madam, sir.

Milos goes over to Car A and gets into it. From the right. Topé, Emanou and Fodère arrive, running, and even more terrified than before. The police whistles are close behind them. Topé, Emanou and Fodère grab the hammocks and take refuge behind them, near Car 1. They hide behind the hammocks. They can't be seen but the extremities of their three instruments can be seen, pointing upwards like three guns. Suddenly Fodère raises his head, looks towards the right, and, horrified, lowers his head. The police whistles are coming nearer right. But just as they are about to enter a voice brings the policemen to a standstill.

DILA'S VOICE *(lasciviously).* Listen to me a moment. Look. *As the sound of footsteps has ceased, we assume that the policemen have stopped.*

Look at that! *(In a plaintive and voluptuous voice.)* I don't know what's come over me. *(Dila bursts into lascivious laughter.)* Do you like it?

Lascivious laughter from Dila. The policemen laugh stupidly. Some of them roar.

Curtain

ACT TWO

Same place. Some hours later. Left, each in a hammock, Emanou, Topé and Fodère are asleep, each one holding his respective instrument. Noises come from Car 2.

MAN'S VOICE. Once and for all, *are* you going to keep quiet?

TIOSSODO'S VOICE. Please excuse us, sir, we aren't doing it on purpose.

LASCA'S VOICE. It's so small here.

A giggle. Soon Dila enters, right. She goes over to Emanou. She wakes him up.

EMANOU *(with a start)*. Dila. *(Pause.)* So they've finally left you alone?

DILA. Yes.

Topé and Fodère wake up.

TOPÉ. Were they very awful?

DILA. No. Only moderately.

EMANOU. If you hadn't helped us we'd have been caught by now.

DILA. You had a narrow escape. They were so furious.

TOPÉ. What are they going to do to us?

DILA. It's Emanou they want to catch. That's what they said.

Topé. Naturally, you always put yourself in the limelight.

Emanou. Well, it isn't the least bit funny.

Dila. They've even promised a big reward to anyone who tells them where you're hiding.

Emanou. Have they?

Dila. I told you they have. *(Pause.)* I was very tempted to give you away because then I'd have been able to buy myself some sanitary towels.

Emanou. Why didn't you?

Dila *(astonished)*. Oh! Well—I really can't tell you.

Topé. You never know anything.

Dila. I think you ought to know. They may come back.

Emanou. We'll never have any peace with all this going on.

Milos, with a ferocious look, examines the group, his head at the door of Car A. They don't notice him. While he watches them Milos sips a huge bowl of soup, making a great deal of noise. The soup must be very hot because he keeps blowing on it.

Topé. And where on earth can we hide?

Dila. Over here—it's simple.

Topé. They've really got it in for you.

Dila. I really don't understand why. You wouldn't hurt a fly.

Emanou *(looking ashamed)*. Oh, yes, I would. I kill them.

Dila *(couldn't be more astonished)*. Could you really do that?

EMANOU *(apologetically)*. Well—now and then.

DILA. And do you always kill flies?

EMANOU. No : sometimes I kill other things.

DILA. And people too?

EMANOU. Yes, but not much. Except when I see a real bastard—then I kill him.

DILA *(enthusiastically)*. What an extraordinary chap you are! And just to think that you never told me. Aren't you artful! You'd just as soon kill a person as a fly.

EMANOU. It isn't that I'm specially good at it, it's more of a habit.

DILA. And what do you do with the corpses?

EMANOU. I bury them.

DILA. All by yourself?

EMANOU. Yes, all by myself. My father taught me when I was little that it's better to do things yourself than to have someone to help you, who doesn't know what he's doing.

DILA *(enthusiastically)*. What a marvellous chap you are! Aren't you artful!

EMANOU. And then I go and look at the will-o'-the-wisps at night—they're so pretty.

DILA. At night?

EMANOU. Yes, at night. They're so pretty! And then on All Saints' Day I put geraniums on their graves and I play the trumpet to them.

DILA. Aren't you kind to the dead!

EMANOU (*modestly*). Oh, it's nothing.

DILA (*suddenly*). That may well be why the cops are looking for you.

EMANOU. No, they're looking for me because I play the trumpet. You know very well that they're furious because I play the trumpet for the poor.

TOPÉ. I think the best thing we can do is to hide as quickly as possible.

DILA. Topé's right.

They get up.

EMANOU. Good-bye, Dila.

TOPÉ. Good-bye, Dila.

DILA. Good-bye.

Fodère, Topé and Emanou go out, left. Dila goes over to Car 1 and puts her head between the folds of the sackcloth curtain.

DILA. Kiss me. (*Kiss.*) Thank you.

Milos, more furious than ever, comes out of Car A. He goes over to Dila. He grabs her by the hair and throws her to the ground.

MILOS (*violently*). What were you doing? (*Silence.*) You thought I wasn't looking, didn't you? (*Silence.*) Whore! Bloody whore! The one thing you dream of is to kiss the first person you come across. (*Pause.*) Get up.

Dila picks herself up.

Your hand.

Dila holds out her hand. Milos hits her on the fingers. Laughter is heard from the cars.

And again.

As before.

You know how jealous I am. Ask me to forgive you.

DILA. Forgive me.

MILOS. On your knees—and say it better than that.

DILA *(on her knees)*. Forgive me.

Laughter is heard from the cars.

MILOS. And don't do it again. Let's go.

Milos puts his arm affectionately round Dila. They go into Car A together. Sounds are heard in Car 2.

TIOSSODO'S VOICE. It's time to get up, Lasca.

LASCA'S VOICE. Just one more minute.

TIOSSODO'S VOICE. Neither one minute nor two. Do you hear me?

LASCA'S VOICE. Just a tiny little snooze.

Tiossodo comes out of Car 2; he is wearing a policeman's uniform. He pulls Lasca out with some force; she is also dressed in police uniform, like Tiossodo. They both have whistles round their necks. Lasca is half asleep.

TIOSSODO *(doing exercises: arms crossed, flexing his legs)*. One, two, one, two, one, two, one, two, one two. *(He suddenly notices that Lasca isn't following suit. He says to her brutally.)* But what are you doing? Get started.

Lasca reluctantly does the same exercises as Tiossodo.

One, two, one, two, one, two, one, two, one, two . . .

Topé enters right. He watches Lasca and Tiossodo doing their exercises.

LASCA. Have we nearly finished? I'm very tired.

TIOSSODO *(angry)*. You're very sensitive today. Next exercise.

Flexing the trunk: they touch their toes with their hands without bending their knees.

One, two, one, two, one, two, one, two, one, two. . . .

Lasca can't manage to touch her toes with her hands. Tiossodo suddenly notices this.

What? You can't touch your toes? Just do it for a moment and let me watch you. *(Tiossodo watches her, saying.)* One, two, one, two, one, two, one, two. . . . Come on, try. You wouldn't be as supple as a board, by any chance? One, two, one, two, one, two. More energy! One, two, one, two, one, two, one, two. . . .

Topé goes up to Tiossodo and Lasca.

TOPÉ *(to Tiossodo)*. Are you a policeman?

Milos puts his head out of the window of Car A and watches what is going on with the help of a monocle. He looks very pleased.

TIOSSODO. At your service.

TOPÉ. Are you looking for Emanou?

At the name of Emanou, Tiossodo and Lasca start in surprise.

TIOSSODO. Of course.

TOPÉ. Is there a reward for the person who tells you where he's hiding?

TIOSSODO. Yes.

TOPÉ. I'll take you there. He's with his friend Fodère.

TIOSSODO. And how shall we know which one is Emanou?

TOPÉ. Oh, that's simple; when I get there I'll kiss one of them. And that one will be Emanou.

TIOSSODO. Come with us. You can tell us where he is.

LASCA. Ready?

TIOSSODO. Ready.

Lasca and Tiossodo both crouch down in the position the athlete takes at the start of the 100 Metres.

LASCA. On your marks, are you ready, get set. . . .

Lasca doesn't have time to say "go". Some moments previously a hand has appeared out of Car 1. The hand is holding a pistol. Just when Lasca is about to say "go" the pistol is fired. Lasca and Tiossodo go out left at top speed. Topé stays behind for a moment, somewhat disconcerted, but then he darts off after them, also at top speed.
Milos continues to look through his monocle. Then he calmly puts down the monocle and looks towards the left with minute opera glasses, then with field glasses, and finally with a telescope which he extends little by little. He tries

very hard to see what is going on. But it is clear that, in spite of the trouble he takes, he can't manage it. Milos goes back into Car A.
In Car 3 a candle is lit. A gleam of light can be seen through the sackcloth curtain.

MAN'S VOICE. He's forgotten us again.

WOMAN'S VOICE. Yes, he must have. At this hour!

MAN'S VOICE. I can't hold it any longer.

WOMAN'S VOICE. Nor can I.

MAN'S VOICE. Shall I call him?

WOMAN'S VOICE. Leave him, you know how touchy he is. If he realises that he's forgotten he'll get in a rage.

MAN'S VOICE. But I *can't* any longer. I'm going to call him.

Sound of a horn. Milos comes out of Car A, and goes over to Car 3. He puts his head under the sackcloth curtain.

MILOS. Can I get you something, sir?—Madam?

MAN'S VOICE. Hm. D'you know what time it is?

MILOS *(takes an alarm clock out of his pocket and looks at it horrified).* It's not possible! Please excuse my deplorable forgetfulness. I can't tell you how deeply I regret. . . . I will be back immediately.

Milos goes over to Car A. He goes into it. Murmurs are heard—Milos and Dila are arguing in whispers. Shortly afterwards Dila comes out holding a gigantic chamber pot. She is in her slip—she has just got out of bed—and she is very sleepy. She goes over to Car 3. She hands in the chamber pot between the sackcloth curtains.

DILA. Good evening. Here you are.

Soon two people are heard urinating at the same time in the same receptacle inside Car 3. Every now and then they sigh with satisfaction. Milos comes out of Car A with a glass of water on a tray. The people in Car 3 have finished urinating. The chamber pot appears through the sackcloth curtain. Dila takes it again.

DILA. Thank you very much.

Immediately after, Milos gives the glass of water to the man in Car 5.

MILOS. Good evening, sir. Here is your water.

Dila takes the chamber pot to Car 2.

DILA. Good evening, sir. Here you are.

MAN'S VOICE. What d'you expect me to do with *that*?

DILA. It's your usual time, sir.

MAN'S VOICE. I tell you I haven't any to do.

They have a little struggle. Dila tries to put the pot through the curtains of Car 2. It is clear that the man is vigorously resisting this. Dila wins. The man in Car 2, grumbling, very cross, produces four drops and a tiny stream. He hands the pot out.

DILA. Thank you, sir.

MILOS *(furiously, having taken the glass away from Car 5, to Dila)*. You've made a mistake again! I've told you a thousand times, it isn't that one you have to give it to but the other one. *(He points to Car 4.)* D'you hear me? How many times do I have to tell you?

DILA. I'm sorry. I didn't do it on purpose.

MILOS. I didn't do it on purpose! D'you think that's a good excuse?

Dila passes the pot between the curtains of Car 4.

DILA. Here you are, sir.

He is heard urinating a little. He gives back the pot which appears between the curtains. Dila goes to get it.

MAN'S VOICE *(he keeps hold of the pot).* A bit more—just a moment. *(He is heard urinating. He gives back the pot. Dila goes to get it. He keeps it once more.)* A bit more. Just a moment. *(He is heard urinating again. He finally hands the pot to Dila.)* Thank you.

Dila hesitates with the pot in her hand.

DILA. Can I go to bed now, I'm terribly sleepy?

MILOS. Yes. Off you go. I'm sleepy too. But empty it first.

Dila goes into the wings. She is heard emptying the contents of the pot. She comes back, the pot in her hand, still hesitating. Milos puts his arm round her lovingly. They both get into Car A. Silence.
Emanou and Fodère enter right. They cross the stage from right to left. They both look around them intently.

EMANOU. To-pé! To-pé! *(Pause.)* Where are you, Topé? *(Pause.)* To-pé!

Fodère lifts up the curtains of Car 3. The horrified scream of a woman is heard. They have surprised her in the nude. Suitable gestures from Fodère. They move over to the left. They go out left. Emanou can be heard in the distance, calling.

Topé! Topé!

Lasca and Tiossodo enter, right, pushing a bicycle. They hold it by the handlebars. They cross the stage from right to left very quickly. When they are just about to go off, left, they stop. They wait for a moment, looking towards the right. Topé appears, exhausted. He has obviously been trying to keep close on their heels but not been able to.

LASCA *(to Topé)*. When are we going to find this famous Emanou?

Milos appears at the window, looking pleased; he watches them with his monocle.

TOPÉ. I thought he was there. *(He points to a vague spot behind the cars)*. We'll see if I find him on our next round.

TIOSSODO AND LASCA *(astonished and horrified, they look at Topé)*. Have we got to go round again?

TOPÉ. We'll have to if we want to get hold of him.

TIOSSODO *(profoundly sad)*. Once more round!

LASCA *(sad as well, but looking for a solution)*. But it's only once more. . . .

TIOSSODO *(heroically)*. Let us do our duty, no matter what it costs us.

They immediately go out, left, at top speed. Topé, exhausted, tries to follow them, he gets left a long way behind.
Milos goes to Car 2 and knocks on the door. He and the man from Car 2 whisper through the curtain. Every so often they roar with laughter. Milos goes back to Car A and takes his field glasses out of it. He focuses them on the audience to see if they're working properly. He goes back to Car

2. Whispers, laughter. He gives the glasses to the man in Car 2. More laughter. Suddenly a voice comes from Car 4.

MAN'S VOICE *(Car 4).* I want some, too.

Milos goes over to Car 4. He whispers to the man inside it. Laughter. Milos goes to Car A and takes another pair of glasses out of it. He focuses them on the audience to test them. He goes back to Car 4. Whispers. Laughter. He gives him the glasses. Whispers. Laughter. Suddenly Milos looks towards the right and seems pleased. He goes over to Car 2 on tiptoe. He puts his head through the curtains.

MILOS. Here they come!

Giggles. He goes over to Car 4 on tiptoe. As before. Here they come!

Giggles. Milos hides behind Car A. You can't see that his head is turned towards the right. Field glasses appear between the sackcloth curtains of Cars 2 and 4—one pair in each car. Laughter. Shortly afterwards, Fodère and Emanou enter. They cross the stage from right to left. The two pairs of glasses follow them as they move.

EMANOU. To-pé! To-pé! To-pé ...

They go out left. Their voices can be heard in the distance, calling; To-pé! To-pé!...
As soon as they go off, more laughter is heard from Cars 2 and 4. Milos' boisterous laugh is heard. Milos looks towards the right. Great satisfaction. He goes over to Cars 2 and 4. He says to the people, inside them.

MILOS. Here come the others, now.

Milos again hides behind Car A. The glasses are now turned towards the right. Suddenly Lasca and Tiossodo enter, at top speed, pushing a bicycle that they hold by the handle-

*bars. They cross the stage from right to left. A few minutes
after they have disappeared, left, Topé enters, right, completely exhausted. He is clearly still trying to catch up Lasca
and Tiossodo. He crosses the stage from right to left and
goes out, left. The glasses in Cars 2 and 4 have followed
Lasca and Tiossodo, and then Topé, as they cross the stage.
When Topé has gone out, laughter is heard from Cars 2
and 4 and also from Milos.*

MILOS *(going over to Car 2, to the man inside)*. They're
just kids.

MAN'S VOICE *(Car 2)*. Yes, they're real kids. *(He laughs.)*

MILOS *(aloud, speaking to the people behind the scenes)*.
No, really though, did you take a good look at them?
(Laughs.) It was so funny.

*He laughs, and is imitated by the people in the cars so that
the laughter becomes continuous and for half a minute all
that can be heard is this collective crescendo. Suddenly Dila
appears at the window of Car A. She is very angry.*

DILA. There you are again, laughing like half-wits.

*All of a sudden, dead silence. Milos tries to hide—he is terri-
fied.*

What was making you laugh so much?

Silence. Slight whispers from the cars.

And now you're silent.

MILOS. Let them be, Dila, don't be cross with them. They're
asleep, they won't hear you.

*When Milos started speaking, the man in Car 2 put his
glasses through the curtains. He turns them blatantly on
Dila.*

DILA. Asleep are they? D'you think I was born yesterday? A minute ago they were laughing like imbeciles and then, hey presto, they're asleep. Do you take me for an idiot?

MILOS. They weren't laughing. They were dreaming. You know very well that the poor things have so many nightmares that they're crying out all night long.

DILA. I tell you they were laughing.

MILOS. One often doesn't hear very well. How many times have I thought they were calling out when in fact they were laughing! And how many times the opposite! The poor things, they suffer so much!

Dila suddenly notices that the glasses in Car 2 are directed on her.

DILA *(indignant, to the man in Car 2)*. How dare you watch me through your glasses?

The man in Car 2 immediately pulls back his glasses. At this precise moment the man in Car 4 blatantly puts his through the curtains and watches Dila.

MILOS. What glasses?

DILA. Didn't you see them?

MILOS. Of course not, the poor man is quite simply fast asleep!

DILA *(suddenly noticing the glasses of the man in Car 4)*. And you too, now? You're getting going with your glasses as well?

The man hurriedly withdraws them while at the same time they appear and disappear in Car 2.

MILOS. Let them be, Dila. If you keep on telling them off they'll be offended. You know how shy and touchy they are.

DILA. How dare you take their side? When you're the worst of the whole lot.

MILOS. Dila, calm down, and let's go to bed.

DILA. I'll deal with you tomorrow.

MILOS. No, Dila, don't do that, don't punish me.

DILA. Yes, I shall; I *shall* punish you. You've certainly deserved it.

MILOS. Just look what you're like with me!

DILA. Come to bed and stop grumbling. I'm too good to you.

Dila and Milos go into Car A. During this last scene the glasses in Cars 2 and 4 have alternately been trained on Dila. As Dila is about to shut the door of Car A, the two pairs of glasses follow her at the same time. Silence. The glasses disappear. From Car 3, the following conversation between husband and wife is heard.

WOMAN'S VOICE. She really is cruel to us.

MAN'S VOICE. One of these days she'll even forbid us to breathe.

WOMAN'S VOICE. What have we done to her to make her like that to us?

MAN'S VOICE. When we've always been nice to her.

WOMAN'S VOICE. When she hears what we've done she'll have a fit.

MAN'S VOICE. No doubt about that.

WOMAN'S VOICE. She's annoyed with us.

MAN'S VOICE. She can't stand us any longer.

WOMAN'S VOICE. She certainly can't.

Silence. Soon Emanou and Fodère enter, right. They go towards the left. They call "To-pé! To-pé!" They look for him. When they reach the middle of the stage, Fodère motions to Emanou to sit down on the hammocks. They sit down. They half lie on the hammocks. They look tired. They fall asleep. Suddenly, grunts are heard in Car 3. Silence.

MAN'S VOICE *(Car 1)*. They've certainly asked for it. *Silence.*

MAN'S VOICE *(Car 2)*. But they could have avoided it, all the same.

Silence.

MAN'S VOICE *(Car 3)*. Avoided it? *(Silence.)*

WOMAN'S VOICE *(Car 3)*. That's easy to say, but. . . .

Silence.

MAN'S VOICE *(Car 4)*. They haven't had enough experience.

Silence.

MAN'S VOICE *(Car 5)*. They're just kids!

Silence. All of a sudden, from all five cars weighty, sober, ponderous discussions start, without a single voice being raised. As they are all talking at the same time and more or less in the same moderate tone of voice, practically nothing can be heard. From time to time scraps of sentences can be made out: "What I think is. . . ." "We couldn't have done anything else. . . ." "In a case like that. . . ." "But maybe it's a question of. . . ." "But rather that than. . . ." "That's why if there were any means. . . ." "What I say is. . . ." The man in Car 3 is now heard shouting: "Silence, silence, silence." His voice rises in a crescendo until everyone has stopped talking. Silence. The field glasses appear in Cars 2 and 4 and are turned on Car 3. A horn is sounded in Car 3. Dila comes out of Car A carrying a pot full of hot water. She passes it through the curtains of Car 3. Then she gets into Car 3. Noises inside it. Finally the cries of a new-born child are heard. Whispers in the other cars. Giggles.

MAN'S VOICE *(Car 3)*. What is it?

DILA'S VOICE. A boy.

MAN'S VOICE. A boy! Just what I wanted. It's so difficult to get girls married. A boy! It's a boy! *(He's crazy with joy.)*

Whispers in the other cars.

DILA'S VOICE *(angrily)*. And let that be the last time!

MAN'S VOICE. We didn't do it on purpose. We took precautions.

DILA'S VOICE *(angrily)*. Precautions! The thing is, you're real swine. The moment one turns one's back there you are on top of one another. Let this be the very last time!

MAN'S VOICE. Yes, I promise you it will.

Whispers. Giggles. Dila comes out of Car 3. She goes back to Car A. She disappears inside it. Silence, except that the cries of the new-born child are occasionally heard. Emanou wakes up. He wakes up Fodère.

EMANOU. And Topé is still not back! Where on earth can he have got to? *(Mime from Fodère indicating hesitation.)* It's beginning to worry me.

Fodère makes a sign to Emanou that they should play their instruments.

EMANOU. That's an idea—then he'll realise that we're here.

Emanou plays his trumpet and Fodère his saxophone. They both play with enthusiasm. Soon Lasca and Tiossodo enter, right, still dressed in police uniform and still pushing the bicycle by the handlebars. Lasca and Tiossodo cross the stage at top speed while Emanou and Fodère go on playing. When she gets to the middle of the stage, Lasca turns round and looks into the distance, right, with great difficulty. She holds her hand over her eyes to protect them.

LASCA *(to Tiossodo)*. He can't move an inch.

TIOSSODO. It doesn't matter. We must go on.

They cross the stage and go out, left. Fodère and Emanou are still playing. Soon Lasca and Tiossodo come back and make a sign to Fodère and Emanou which means: don't play so loudly and don't annoy us with all that racket. Emanou and Fodère play less loudly. Lasca and Tiossodo immediately go out very quickly, left. Emanou and Fodère go on playing. Finally they stop playing.

MAN'S VOICE *(Car 2)*. Thank goodness they've stopped!

MAN'S VOICE *(Car 4)*. That's quite enough for today.

Emanou and Fodère look all around them. They are upset because Topé still doesn't come.

EMANOU. Not a sign. He's not there. It looks as if he's lost.

Fodère makes a sign to Emanou indicating that they should consult Dila.

The poor thing, she must be asleep.

Fodère insists.

Right, I'll go and tell her.

Emanou knocks at the door of Car A. He says, trying not to speak too loudly: "Dila, Dila, Dila." Milos appears at the window of Car A.

MILOS. Do you gentlemen want to stay the night?

EMANOU. No. We want to talk to Dila.

MILOS. You want a woman, gentlemen. Do you prefer Dila or a brunette?

EMANOU. We want to talk to Dila.

MILOS *(still respectful)*. As you wish, gentlemen, I'll call Dila at once. *(Milos gets back into the car.)*

MILOS' VOICE. Don't dress, I tell you. Go out naked. *(Pause.)* That's right, obstinate as usual.

Dila comes out of the car completely dressed.

EMANOU. Dila!

DILA. What d'you want?

EMANOU. We're looking for Topé. Do you know where he is?

DILA. I haven't seen him. Wasn't he with you?

EMANOU. Yes, but he's disappeared.

DILA. Well I haven't seen Topé any more than the man in the moon.

EMANOU. We're in a fine mess: the cops are looking for us and Topé isn't even with us.

DILA. That's true.

EMANOU. What do you think the cops will do to me?

DILA. They're bound to kill you. You know very well that that lot always do things in a big way.

EMANOU. If Topé was here I wouldn't feel so alone.

DILA. That's reasonable.

EMANOU. I shall really be frightened.

DILA. Come on now, you mustn't. And anyway you knew very well when you started playing the trumpet for the poor that it would all come to a bad end.

EMANOU. But I didn't think I was doing any harm.

DILA. No, but you went on too long. One day or two, that would have been all right, but no more.

EMANOU. Yes, of course, I realise now; I set a bad example.

DILA. A very bad example. Just think what would happen if everyone took it into his head to be good like you.

EMANOU. You're right; it wouldn't do at all.

DILA. And the pullovers and the daisies. . . . It doesn't even make any difference if you do these things in secret, they always come out in the end.

EMANOU. Yes, but you know very well that when we're good *(he recites this hesitatingly)* we experience a great joy . . . *(he continues to recite, hesitating more and more)* . . . that . . . springs from . . . no, that comes from . . . from the peace . . . from the goodness, no, from the goodness, no, from the peace . . . that. . . . *(normal voice, tragically.)* I've forgotten it, Dila.

DILA *(disagreeably surprised)*. What—you've forgotten it?

EMANOU. Yes, Dila. I've forgotten it. It's not my fault, I didn't do it on purpose.

Suddenly, back right, the shouts of a crowd are heard: "They're always looking for an excuse." "They've made fun of us quite enough." "Mu-sic! Mu-sic! Mu-sic! . . ." Emanou and Fodère listen to the protests, scared stiff.

EMANOU. D'you hear them? *(Pause.)* They sound furious!

DILA. Of course, and it's your fault. You promise them you'll go and then you don't.

EMANOU. But I can't, Dila. If I go, the cops will arrest me.

Protests can still be heard at the back: "Mu-sic! Mu-sic! Mu-sic!" becomes the angry people's chorus.

DILA. If you like, I'll go and tell them to be quiet.

EMANOU. Yes, Dila, do. I don't dare.

Dila goes out, right. Two things happen at the same time: (a) Back right, they boo Dila. Her voice is heard in the distance.

DILA's VOICE. Just keep quiet for a moment. *(Silence.)* The musicians can't come. The police are after them. *(They hiss, they shout; "That's just excuses" "We've had enough, etc.")* Be quiet. *(Silence. Violently.)* Go away at once if you don't want me to get really angry. *(Murmurs.)* Did you hear me? Go away once and for all, and without another word. *(Silence.)*

(b) Tiossodo and Lasca come in, right. They are walking very quickly and hold the bicycle by the handlebars. They stop in the middle of the stage. They look back and right.

LASCA. He can't put one foot in front of the other. He's on his knees.

TIOSSODO *(very pleased)*. We're already a whole lap ahead of him.

Lasca and Tiossodo go out, left, still at full speed. Dila enters, right.

DILA. It looks as if they've calmed down.

EMANOU. Thank goodness.

DILA *(reprimanding him)*. What you should do is never go back on what you tell them.

EMANOU. You'll see, it's the last time.

DILA. I haven't the slightest confidence in your promises.

EMANOU. You're all against me.

DILA. But you behave like a child, without thinking. Who asked you to get yourself in such a mess? You just asked for it. Do you think anyone with a little experience and the minimum of intelligence would have behaved like you have?

EMANOU. That's the way I am. I can't behave in any other way.

DILA. You can't behave in any other way; but what about other people, though?

EMANOU. Perhaps I'm weaker than they are.

DILA. Weakness looks like weakness to me.

EMANOU. You all reproach me.

DILA. Do you think you deserve anything else? And anyway, as if that wasn't enough, now you've even gone and forgotten why people should be good.

EMANOU. You'll see; it'll come back to me.

DILA. You forget everything. You used to know how to act in a circus, but now you've forgotten. You only know how to play the trumpet now, and we have to count ourselves lucky that you can still do that.

Topé enters, right. He is exhausted. He goes over to one of the hammocks when he has greeted his friends, and lies down, overcome by fatigue.

EMANOU. Topé! Where'd you got to?

TOPÉ. And you?

EMANOU. Were you looking for us?

TOPÉ. Yes.

EMANOU. We were looking for you, too.

DILA. That's why you didn't meet.

EMANOU. You do look tired!

TOPÉ. Of course I am. I've been doing nothing but run since I left you. Funny sort of race!

EMANOU. Poor Topé!

DILA. Well now, *he* knows very well how to behave in life. You ought to take notice of what he says.

EMANOU. I've got some almonds. Would you like to have some with me?

They all nod. Emanou brings out a packet of almonds. Each in turn plunges his hand into the bag and starts to eat.

DILA. They're very good.

EMANOU. Guess where I took them from!

DILA. From the confectioner's in the square.

EMANOU. You're very intelligent.

DILA. I know you so well: you tell yourself that he's a bastard and that he's very rich and so that excuses your pinching a packet of almonds from him every evening.

EMANOU. Well, if I do, it's so that there are some for everyone, without thinking there's any harm in it.

DILA. You do everything without thinking there's any harm in it.

EMANOU. And anyway you know very well that his shop is chock-full of stuff; what difference can it make to him?

They all eat with an air of great enjoyment.

DILA. D'you know something? If the cops finally get you, later on, every time we eat almonds we'll remember you, and that you used to steal them for us every night.

TOPÉ. We'll imagine we're giving you some.

Fodère gaily makes a sign of assent. The cries of the new-
born child in Car 3 are heard through the silence. Then its
mother is heard saying: "Now who's going to feed her little
darling?" The mother gives it the breast and the cries fade
away.
During the silence the three friends have been eating voraci-
ously. Every now and then they remark "They're salted."
or "Delicious," etc.

DILA. I could easily eat a couple of pounds all by myself.

Lasca and Tiossodo enter, right, holding the bicycle by the
handlebars. They are still in police uniform and walking
quickly. They go towards the left. Suddenly they notice
Topé with the others. When Topé sees them he goes over
to Emanou and kisses him. Lasca and Tiossodo watch him
and then immediately throw themselves on Emanou.

LASCA *(to Emanou)*. Are you Emanou?

EMANOU. Yes, that's me.

LASCA. You're under arrest.

Dila rushes out, frightened to death, and takes refuge, right.
Lasca tries to handcuff Emanou. Tiossodo watches her.

TOPÉ *(trying to get her attention while she's handcuffing*
Emanou). My money, give me my money. *(Pause.)* You
promised to pay me. *(Pause.)* I was the one who denounced
him, you ought to give me my money. *(Pause.)* You promised.
Don't you remember?

Lasca has had some difficulty in handcuffing Emanou. She
couldn't get the lock to work. All this time Topé was de-
manding his money. Neither Lasca nor Tiossodo pay the

slightest attention to him. Finally, when the handcuffs are properly fixed, Lasca says to Tiossodo.

LASCA. Have you got the cheque on you?

TIOSSODO. No, *I* haven't got it. What should *I* be doing with it?

LASCA. But you had it, didn't you?

TIOSSODO. No, I didn't. Have a good look in your things.

Topé continues to demand his money, more and more insistently. Neither Lasca nor Tiossodo has looked at him once. Lasca searches in her pockets; she pulls out all sorts of things—bits of paper, pencils, flowers, toy whistles, handkerchiefs, a jack-in-the-box, etc. Tiossodo, in his excess of zeal, opens the box by mistake; the figure springs up in his face. Lasca goes on looking for the cheque. Topé, getting more and more anxious, demands his money.

TIOSSODO. No, have a *proper* look.

They go on looking.

LASCA *(thinking).* Ah! *(She taps herself on the forehead.)* What a head I've got! *(She takes off her cap. She looks inside it. She takes out a piece of paper. To Topé, very scornfully.)* Here, take your cheque.

She holds it out to him without looking at him. Topé, terribly pleased, jumps up and down. He says: "Hip, hip, hip, hurrah!". He dashes out, left, beside himself with joy.

TIOSSODO. Aren't you a scatterbrain.

LASCA. Yes, I am; I forget everything.

Suddenly Lasca and Tiossodo notice that Fodère is looking at them—Fodère had moved a little way off while they were

*handcuffing Emanou, he didn't want them to see him, but
he wanted to watch what was going on. Tiossodo brutally
grabs hold of Fodère by the lapels.*

TIOSSODO *(to Lasca, pointing to Fodère).* He was with him.
Wasn't he?

LASCA. Yes, I think I saw him with him.

TIOSSODO. Wasn't he the one who used to play the saxophone with Emanou?

LASCA. Yes, I think he was.

TIOSSODO *(to Fodère).* You were Emanou's friend, weren't
you?

*Fodère shakes his head. He makes sweeping gestures of inno-
cence.*

LASCA *(to Fodère).* Were you *really* not his friend?

*Fodère shakes his head. He makes sweeping gestures of inno-
cence.*

TIOSSODO *(to Fodère).* Just the same I could have sworn
I'd seen you with him. Aren't you a friend of his?

*Fodère shakes his head. He protests his innocence more than
ever with his head.*

LASCA. Well, if he says he wasn't . . .

*Tiossodo lets go of Fodère. Fodère, very scared, runs off,
left. Suddenly all the horns sound at once.*

Shall we take him to the lamp post? *(She points to her right.)*

TIOSSODO. Yes, that's the best place.

LASCA. Have you got the whips?

TIOSSODO. Of course I have.

LASCA *(brutally to Emanou)*. Keep still !

Tiossodo knocks gently and ceremoniously at the door of Car A. Milos immediately appears at the window. Milos looks at Tiossodo and disappears behind the sackcloth curtain. He reappears with a basin and a jug of water. Tiossodo ceremoniously washes his hands. Milos again disappears. Tiossodo, with his hands wet, knocks at the door of Car 2. Shortly afterwards a towel appears between the folds of the curtain.
While this has been going on Lasca has been carefully measuring Emanou and examining him in detail. No doubt this is necessary, and she carries out her task conscientiously. All this in absolute silence.

LASCA. Are you ready?

TIOSSODO. Just a minute! *(He does a few limbering-up exercises.)* Now I'm ready.

LASCA. Let's go, then.

Lasca gives Emanou a push. All three move off towards the right, first Emanou, and behind him Tiossodo, and Lasca, who is still holding the bicycle by the handlebars. They go out, right. Laughter is immediately heard coming from the five cars. Soon afterwards Tiossodo's voice is heard in the distance, right.

TIOSSODO'S VOICE. I'll start.

Sounds of the whip, and Emanou's groans. In Car 3 the cries of the new-born baby are heard, which cover up Emanou's groans.

WOMAN'S VOICE. *(Car 3)*. What's the matter with my little darling? Don't cry.

The baby cries more and more loudly.

Amuse him.

MAN'S VOICE *(Car 3)*. I don't know how to. I don't know how to make faces at babies.

WOMAN'S VOICE. But don't you realise that the poor little thing is crying? Aren't you sorry for him? Try and amuse him.

MAN'S VOICE *(braying very loudly)*. Hee-haw! Hee-haw! Hee-haw!

The child cries even more. Milos comes out of Car A, still impeccably dressed in his manservant's uniform, carrying a baby's bottle on a tray. When he gets to Car 3 he hands the bottle in.

MILOS. Here you are, sir, madam.

The child stops crying. In the silence the sounds of Emanou being whipped can be heard in the distance. His groans get louder. Suddenly a sharp cry from Emanou. The child in Car 3 starts crying again. His parents try to quieten him. Sound of a horn from Car 2. Milos puts his head through the curtain of Car 2.

MAN'S VOICE *(Car 2)*. Bring me the child. I want to see it.

Milos goes back to Car 3. He puts his hand through the curtain and gets hold of the newly-born child which is wrapped in swaddling-clothes. He carries it over to Car 2. The child is still crying.

MAN'S VOICE *(Car 2)*. Cheer up, little one. *(The child stops crying.)* It looks like a monkey. You can cry, little one. *(The child starts yelling.)* Not so loud. *(The child cries less loudly.)* Be quiet, little one. *(The child is silent.)* He seems to be obedient.

MILOS *(confidentially)*. He's like his father. He's the spitting image of his father.

MAN'S VOICE. Does his father look like a monkey, too?

MILOS. No, what I mean is that he's very obedient, too.

MAN'S VOICE. You can cry, little one. *(The child cries.)* Louder, little one. *(The child cries more loudly.)* He's really very obedient, this child. You can take him back to his mother.

MILOS. Thank you very much, sir. Is there anything else you wish, sir?

Milos goes over to Car 3. He gives the child back.

WOMAN'S VOICE *(Car 3)*. Carry him about a bit so he goes to sleep.

MILOS. Would you like me to sing him a lullaby to make him go to sleep quickly?

WOMAN'S VOICE. No, not a lullaby. Our child is a real soldier. Sing him the dragoons' march.

MILOS. With drums or with trumpets?

WOMAN'S VOICE. With drums.

MILOS. At your service, madam.

Milos starts walking about with the child. He rocks him like a nurse. In spite of his promise he sings him a lullaby. While he is walking round with the child, the following conversation is heard in Car 3.

WOMAN'S VOICE. Did you hear what he said?

MAN'S VOICE. Yes, he's charming!

WOMAN'S VOICE. But did you actually hear what he said about the child?

MAN'S VOICE. The business about the monkey?

WOMAN'S VOICE. Yes.

MAN'S VOICE. I've already told you he's charming. I'm sure that he hasn't been able to sleep for pleasure, ever since he heard we've got a child.

WOMAN'S VOICE. He's charming.

Sounds of the whip, and Emanou's groans are heard. A sharp cry from Emanou. The child, still in Milos' arms, cries boisterously. Sound of the horn from Car 4. Milos goes over to Car 4 with the child crying in his arms. He puts his head in through the curtain of Car 4.

MAN'S VOICE *(Car 4)*. Give him to me.

Milos passes the child into Car 4. The man is heard beating the child. The child becomes silent. The man in Car 4 gives the child back to Milos. The child starts crying again.

MAN'S VOICE *(Car 4)*. Pass him in again.

As before.

Give him to me again.

As before. The child stops crying once and for all. Milos starts walking about with the child again, singing it a lullaby. Sound of the horn in Car 3.

WOMAN'S VOICE *(Car 3)*. Pass me the child.

MILOS *(giving her the child)*. Here you are, madam.

WOMAN'S VOICE. Has he been good?

MILOS. Yes, very good.

WOMAN'S VOICE. Has he had a pee?

MILOS. No—I tell you he's been very good.

WOMAN'S VOICE. He's a real little angel.

MILOS. Is there anything else you wish, madam, sir?

WOMAN'S VOICE. No, nothing else.

MILOS. Then I wish you a good night.

Milos goes back to Car A. He gets into it. Sounds of the whip, and Emanou's groans are heard. The whipping stops. Silence.

WOMAN'S VOICE *(Car 3)*. Look, he's sleeping like a little angel.

MAN'S VOICE *(Car 3)*. Like a real little angel.

Both the Man and Woman in Car 3 repeat the words "sleeping like a little angel" over and over again, more and more softly, until nothing more can be heard. Silence.
Tiossodo and Lasca enter, right, holding the bicycle by the handlebars. They seem to be putting a lot of effort into it, they move forward slowly. Emanou, dishevelled, covered in sweat and blood, is tied on to it, the back of his neck is on the handlebars, his feet on the carrier, and his arms are stretched out along the handlebars. They cross the stage from right to left. They stop in the middle. Two things happen:

(a) Dila enters right. She goes up to Emanou with a big cloth and sponges the sweat from his face. When he sees her, Emanou makes one last effort and says:

EMANOU *(reciting)*. When we're good we experience . . . *(a long murmur)* . . . of the peace of spirit . . . *(another murmur)* . . . the ideal man.

Dila kisses him passionately on the mouth and runs away, right.
(b) Tiossodo knocks at the door of Car A. Shortly afterwards, Milos comes out.

TIOSSODO. Help us.

MILOS. I can't, I've got a lot of work to do.

TIOSSODO. I tell you, you're to help us.

MILOS *(with a bad grace)*. All right, come on then.

Milos, Tiossodo and Lasca start to go off. Tiossodo and Lasca hold the bicycle by the handlebars. Milos pushes from behind. Even though there are three of them they have a good deal of trouble. They cross the stage from right to left and go out, left. The field glasses in Cars 2 and 4 have been following them as they go. When the bicycle has gone off, laughter is heard from the cars. A pause. The day dawns. Back right the heart-rending sound of a clarinet and saxophone is heard and continues until the end of the play. Dila comes out of Car A with a small bell in her hand.

DILA *(to all the people in the cars, while she rings the bell violently)*. Get up. Time to get up. *(Violently.)* You needn't pretend to be asleep, I know perfectly well that you're awake. I tell you to get up.

Dila rings the bell inside all the cars, to make a lot of noise.

It's time to get up. Can't you hear me? Get up, all of you.

While Dila is saying all this, Lasca and Tiossodo enter right. Lasca is dressed as an athlete: she is wearing the number 456 on her chest, and looks tired. Tiossodo at her side is indefatigable. He is dressed normally, and marks time with his head. Lasca is moving at the double. They go from right to left.

TIOSSODO. One, two, one, two, one, two, one, two, one, two. . . .

Curtain